Exceptional Customer Service

Handle Customers with Skill and Confidence

Edited by National Press Publications

D1406970

NATIONAL PRESS PUBLICATIONS

A Division of Rockhurst University Continuing Education Center, Inc.
6901 West 63rd Street • P.O. Box 2949 • Shawnee Mission, Kansas 66201-1349
1-800-258-7248 • 1-913-432-7755

Exceptional Customer Service —
Handle Customers with Skill and Confidence

Published by National Press Publications, Inc.
Copyright 2000 by National Press Publications, Inc.
A Division of Rockhurst University Continuing Education Center, Inc.

Printed in the United States of America

3 4 5 6 7 8 9 10

ISBN 1-55852-275-1

Table of Contents

INTRODUCTION

" ... service people are the most important ones in the organization. Without them there is no product, no sales and no profit. Indeed, they are the product."

— J.W. Marriott, Jr., Chairman of the Board
and President, Marriott Corporation

America has shifted from a manufacturing-based economy to a service-based economy. In fact, more than three-quarters of all jobs created in this country over the last decade have been in the service industry. Service accounts for an estimated 60 percent of the gross national product and 70 percent of all jobs in the United States. It is a vital part of our economy and a critical factor in the success of companies today.

Regardless of the product or service, customers can generally choose to do business with several companies. Most will offer similar products at comparable prices. Frequently, the only thing that separates one company from another is service.

As the front-line person in your company who deals with customers on a day-to-day basis, your job — perhaps more than any other — influences the way the customer perceives your company. From the customer's point of view, you are the company. If you are friendly and helpful, the company is perceived as a pleasant and easy place to do business. By the same token, if you are surly and uncooperative, the company is perceived as unfriendly and a place where it is difficult to get what you want. Whether you are competent and effective, or bumbling and inefficient, your actions will reflect accordingly on your company.

Based on your attitude and actions, customers will make a judgment about:

- What kind of people the company employs

- The company's value system

- Whether or not the company practices what it preaches in its advertising

As a customer service employee for your company, you may be responsible for one or more of the following functions: sales, service or problem-solving.

- **Sales.** You are responsible for selling your company's tangible or intangible products. The sales process may take place in person or through telephone contact.

- **Service.** Customers come to your company when they need a particular service. This can involve sales or it can involve filling an order for a customer. For example, if you work for a travel agency, your job is to book customers' travel plans.

- **Problem-solving.** Customers come to you with problems they have experienced in dealing with your company, and it's your job to find a solution. For example, a customer brings you a radio that was purchased in your store which has stopped working. It is your job, through interactions with the customer, to determine an equitable solution: refund the customer's money, replace the item or exchange it for another brand of radio.

Regardless of which role you perform, your main goal is to develop good customer relationships.

The old school of thought was that customer service was the responsibility of the customer service representative or the complaint department. In today's service-driven economy, however, companies have come to realize that customer service is everyone's business. Every individual in a company is either serving a customer or serving someone whose job it is to serve the customer.

Working effectively with customers is not a trait you are born with; it is a skill you must learn. Although it is true that some people are naturally better at working with the public than others, everyone can learn how to communicate with customers and help meet their needs. The key to success in your job is knowing what your customers expect, how to keep them happy and how to deal with them.

As a customer service employee, you come in contact with hundreds of people every day. It can be a challenging, rewarding job or you can find it difficult and impossible. How you view your job will depend on your attitude and the skills you develop to do it better.

As in any job, your attitude about your work will also affect other areas of your life. Therefore, it is important that you are happy with what you do. If your experiences with customers are positive, you will have a positive outlook on your job and it will affect your overall satisfaction with your life. If, on the other hand, they are negative, they will cloud your overall perspective.

Through this handbook you will learn:

- The current condition of service in America today (Chapter 1)

- Characteristics of superstar customer service companies (Chapter 2)

- What customers want and how to keep them happy (Chapter 3)

- How to communicate effectively with customers (Chapter 4)

- How to handle special customers (Chapter 5)

- Ways to handle complaints in such a way that customer loyalty is assured (Chapter 6)

- Essential elements of the customer service representative's job (Chapter 7)

- How to work with your fellow employees to make sure that the customer's experience is pleasant (Chapter 8)

- The role and function of the customer service supervisor (Chapter 9)

- How to pull it all together (Chapter 10)

1 FACTS ABOUT CUSTOMER SERVICE

Research shows that, generally, most people feel good about the products they purchase, but they are not so happy with the service they receive. As a customer service employee, you can change that by understanding a number of basic facts about customer service and how it works in the minds of the customers themselves. These essential facts are presented in this chapter.

If you want to get some perspective on exactly how valuable your job is, consider these facts:

Fact #1: Service is becoming more and more a competitive factor.

Fact #2: Enormous competitive opportunities exist in most industries.

Fact #3: Service improvement starts at the top: managers must "walk their talk." Research and practical experience show that a universal commitment to quality service does not spontaneously ignite in organizations. If senior management truly believes in service, the idea can become contagious. If they don't, it will go nowhere fast — regardless of what they say.

Fact #4: Quality service translates into profit in most industries.

Fact #5: Management must see the profit impact of service in order to take it seriously.

Fact #6: There are only few really excellent service companies.

Fact #7: The longer you're in a service business, the greater the odds you don't understand your customer. Research into customer perceptions reveals hidden concerns, priorities and feelings that point toward a reconceptualization of the service product and a clearer positioning strategy for the service in its marketplace.

Fact #8: Becoming service-oriented is much tougher than most think.

Fact #9: Your employees are your first market. You have to sell them on the service idea or they will never sell it to your customers.

Fact #10: The way your employees feel about themselves and their jobs will always affect their interactions with the customers. If they believe in giving the best service they can, it will show. If they don't, that will also show.

Fact #11: Most service organizations are in a defensive mode, in terms of quality. The customer service department's job is to absorb the customer's anger when the company is at fault. Few firms are truly proactive with respect to customer satisfaction and making amends for errors or poor service. Giving a simple apology is often a lost art in the world of business.

Fact #12: You don't have to buy people off. A sincere apology and correcting the problem immediately should almost always take care of the problem.

Fact #13: Service has more economic impact than most think ... and is worse than most imagine. Many organizations are paying a terribly high price in "opportunity costs" of lost business due to mediocre service.

Fact #14: Many of the problems of poor or mediocre service originate in systems, procedures, policies, rules and regulations. Too often, we blame the front-line people for poor service, when the real problem is systems that don't work or make sense.

Fact #15: You must not ignore obstacles — deal with them directly. Improved service to the customer is non-negotiable.

Fact #16: Managers do not control the quality of the product when the product is service. Although many of them don't realize it, managers can only indirectly affect the quality of service by inspiring and motivating the people on the front line.

Fact #17: Customers may generalize the entire company from one experience.

Fact #18: Your customer relations are only as strong as your weakest employee.

Fact #19: Today's employees are overmanaged and underled.

Fact #20: A business will spend five times as much to acquire a new customer as it does to service an existing one.

Fact #21: There are five levels of service orientation:

- Going out of business

- Hot pursuit of mediocrity

- Surviving ... present and accounted for

- Really trying

- Service as an art form

Fact #22: Even when people know what they are supposed to do, sometimes they forget. That's why they hold church every Sunday. It's also why you have to constantly remind people what your values are (through your actions as well as your words).

Fact #23: If you want your employees to be polite to your customers, you have to be polite to your employees.

Fact #24: If the boss is a crook, you can't expect the employees to be honest.

Fact #25: Ninety-six percent of unhappy customers never let a business know they are unhappy.

Fact #26: For every complaint received by a company, there are actually 26 customers with problems, six of which are serious.

Fact #27: Customers who complain, even if the problem is not resolved, are more likely to do business with the company again than those who don't voice their complaints.

Fact #28: Of those customers who voice their complaints, 54 to 70 percent will do business with the organization in the future if they think their complaint has been resolved. That figure jumps to 95 percent if the customer thinks that complaint has been resolved promptly.

Fact #29: On average, a customer who has a problem with a company will tell nine or 10 people about it. By the same token, he will tell only four or five people about a good experience. A customer who complains about a problem, but has it resolved, tells five people about the treatment he received.

Fact #30: When service is less than desirable, the primary reasons are almost always:

(1) a thorough lack of skill and knowledge about how to manage service

(2) an equally thorough lack of commitment to service quality as an organizational goal

Fact #31: One in four customers is upset enough to stop doing business with a company if he can find a reasonable alternative. However, only 5 percent of them will register a complaint. Of those who do complain, more than 40 percent are unhappy with the action taken to resolve their problem.

Fact #32: If a business loses one customer who normally spends $50 a week, it will experience a $949,000 reduction in sales the following year.

Fact #33: There are Seven Deadly Sins of Service:

- Apathy — a la George Carlin: DILLIGAD (Do I look like I give a d---?)

- The Brushoff: "That's not my department ... "

- Coldness, hostility, curtness, unfriendliness, inconsiderateness or impatience which says, "you're a nuisance ... go away"

- Condescension or a patronizing tone

- Robot-like treatment: "Thank-you-have-a-nice-day — next" syndrome

- Stupid and rigid rules with no discretion by customer service person

- The Runaround: "you'll have to call ... "

Fact #34: A caring organization is also a disciplined one.

Fact #35: You must see the organization through the customers' eyes.

Fact #36: Every employee must understand that his efforts affect the actual life experience of each customer.

Fact #37: Many customer service departments make similar blunders:

- Misreading the customer

- Lack of a clear business focus

- Mixed messages to employees

- "Smile" training rather than substantive problem-solving

- Rapidly changing "solutions"

- Rigor mortis: This is the way it's always been … and will always be

Fact #38: In nursery school, you learned everything you need to know about handling mistakes: acknowledge your mistake, fix it immediately and say you're sorry. It is likely that your customers, like your mom and dad, will forgive you.

1. Which facts about customer service did you find most surprising? (List at least 5)

2. Which facts do you feel your management should pay more attention to? (at least 4)

3. What steps will you take to bring these facts to their attention?

4. Outline the changes you will make in your job based on the facts presented in this chapter.

Reflections

2 CUSTOMER SERVICE SUPERSTARS

What is great service? Who defines it? How do you know it when you deliver it?

Good service is solving a problem — delivering what people expect to receive. *Great* service is getting below the surface of the problem … delivering what no one expects to receive. It is listening, learning, assessing and refining.

Customer service superstars are few and far between. Once found and studied carefully, however, these outstanding organizations share a number of attributes, attitudes and philosophies. In this chapter, those common elements of superstar success will be identified and examined.

Shared Attributes of Customer Service Superstars

1. Recognize that employee relations mirror customer relations. If you are to be outstanding in customer service, you must be outstanding in your employee relationships.

2. A customer-centered focus is created in the minds of employees. The need for satisfied customers is reinforced from an employee's perspective: the customer is the ultimate paymaster.

3. Develop and implement support systems to reinforce expected behaviors.

4. Recognize that everything that happens in an organization has an impact on customer service. Interconnecting support systems are apparent throughout their organizations.

5. Define and implement precise and demanding performance standards — and high performance expectations — to translate concepts into behavior.

6. Train managers, supervisors and employees to reinforce and maintain those desired behaviors once they have been established.

7. Organizations with exceptional call center service carefully define the roles of managers and supervisors in promoting continuous service superiority.

8. Provide tangible and intangible recognition and reward for exemplary behavior. Employees feel important and appreciated.

9. A "shared fate" feeling exists throughout the organization.

   - The employees have a high level of personal respect for the top executives. They trust them and put stock in their word, and feel confident that someone is at the helm who has a clear direction.

   - Employees consider the organization basically a good place to work. They personally identify with the company.

   - Employees feel a sense of mission — a desire to be part of a big undertaking.

   - Employees typically pitch in to help one another. They share information, fill in for each other, and share important news.

10. Monitor the effectiveness of service and personnel policies, practices, programs and procedures with quantitative measures.

11. Provide strong, continuing reinforcement to sustain customer-oriented value systems and management practices.

12. Maintain a total organizational approach that makes quality of service, as perceived by the customer, the number one driving force for the operation of the business.

Five Keys to Superstardom:

1. **Listen to, understand and respond to** — often in unique and creative ways — the evolving needs and constantly shifting expectations of your customers.

2. **Establish a clear vision** of what superior service is, communicate that vision to employees at every level, and ensure that service quality is personally and positively important to everyone in the organization.

3. **Establish concrete standards of service quality** and regularly measure yourself against those standards. Guard against the "acceptable error" mindset by establishing a 100 percent performance goal.

4. **Hire good people, and train them carefully and extensively.** Teach the knowledge and skills to achieve the service standards, then empower them to work on behalf of customers, whether inside or outside the organization.

5. **Recognize and reward service accomplishments**, either individually or as a group effort. Celebrate the successes of employees who go "one step beyond" for their customers.

How the Champions Do It

- Have the basics down pat

- Believe quality drives profit

- Know their customers intimately

- Have a "whatever-it-takes" attitude

- Recover skillfully from inevitable blunders

- Make service happen inside the company as well as outside

- See management as a helper and supporter

- Care about their employees as well as their customers

- Are perpetually unsatisfied with their performance

These paragons of customer service think and talk about their customers a lot. They keep assessing their customers' perceptions on both products and service. These organizations give in, compromise or add value to the customer in dispute situations where the value of goodwill exceeds the economic stake.

Customer service superstars recover conscientiously from blunders or mishandled moments of truth. They make amends to the customer who has received poor treatment — employing a "whatever-it-takes" policy in trying to remedy the situation for a dissatisfied customer or one with a special need. In addition, these firms redesign systems, redeploy resources and turn sacred cows out to pasture when they get in the way of service quality.

Service Excellence Starts at the Top

Customer service superstars have CEOs who embody the philosophy, "If you're not serving the customer, you'd better be serving someone who is."

These CEOs pay close attention to virtually every detail — including:

- Customer complaint logs

- Complaint letters and phone calls

- Reports from mystery shoppers

- Survey data on outside customers, employees, supervisors and managers, and inside customers

- Programs for communicating, accepting and enforcing precise service standards for both internal and external customers

- Service goals and their degree of attainment

- Service budgets

- Productivity per employee

- Sales per employee

- Employment costs as a percent of total costs (increasing? decreasing? stable?)

- Profit per employee

- Costs of service complaints

- Interval between the time a customer registers a complaint and the time it is satisfactorily settled

- Grievances, strikes, sabotage, absenteeism, sit-downs, slowdowns and walkouts

- Whether the best performers receive the highest pay increases, and whether the margin of difference is significant

- Performance appraisal reviews and discussions

- How customer service excellence is rewarded

- Field service and field sales reports

- Development and maintenance of a strong service triangle

    a. Customer-oriented front-line people

    b. Customer friendly systems

    c. Well-conceived strategy for service

What is a Well-conceived Customer Service Strategy?

1. It is nontrivial; it has weight. It is more than simply a "motherhood" statement or slogan. It is concrete and action-oriented.

2. It conveys a concept or a mission which people in the organization understand, relate to and put into action.

3. It offers a critical benefit premise that is important to the customer. It focuses on something the customer is willing to pay for.

4. It differentiates the organization from its competitors in the eyes of the customer.

5. It is simple, easily put into words, and easily explained to the customer.

Evaluating a Possible Service Strategy

- Can it clearly differentiate you and your service product from the customer's other choices? Is the benefit premise behind the strategy clear and compelling?

- Can you commit to it? Is it something all executives can believe in and work to support?

- Can your organization make it work?

- Can you communicate it to your customers in very concrete, selfish terms?

- Can you dramatize it to your organization's managers and employees?

- Can you make it real operationally? Can you make it concrete and experiential for both the employees and the customers?

Twelve Tips for Pursuing Superstar Customer Service Status

1. Create a clear, focused and realistic mission statement.

2. Define who your customers and clients are.

3. Provide services with clarity — and without ambiguity.

4. Provide clear information and encourage communication.

5. Be approachable — ETDBW (easy to do business with).

6. Respond to customers' needs — quickly and thoroughly.

7. Deliver on all promises — and then deliver some extra.

8. Maintain competence at all levels — at all times.

9. Define service standards — then raise them.

10. Give the people who deal with customers the authority to resolve problems.

11. Make everyone in your company responsible to help the customer.

12. Compensate your staff based on the value they contribute — not according to their job title alone.

Conclusion

Great service is an art. The process of assessing what excellent service is — and determining how to deliver it — never stops. A meticulous attention to detail results in a perpetual analysis of quality, performance and standards.

Customer service superstars are committed to continuous improvement … followed by further improvements on those improvements. Service levels are never adequate. Performance expectations continue to rise. "Good enough" is never enough.

How does your organization stack up?

— How well do we understand our customers and their expectations?

— Have we defined our strategy — our mission or goal — in terms of customer expectations?

— Are our delivery systems accessible and approachable? (Designed to make us "easy to do business with" or simply for our own operational convenience?)

— Are our people selected, trained, empowered and rewarded for providing exceptional service to the customer?

— Do my company's advertising messages expertly communicate the service my company has to offer? Are these messages communicated to customers, employees and owners?

— Do my company's image and identity programs result in the effective communication of my company's service strategy to customers, employees and owners?

— Does my company actively and effectively sell the service it has to offer?

— Does my company stand behind its service strategy and the service it provides?

— Do I do everything in my power to live up to my company's advertising slogans and service guarantees? Do I manage my staff toward the same goal?

— Do I believe in the services my company offers, and can I sell them effectively?

Reflections

— Do I take responsibility for informing my staff about changes and new service offerings so they may do their jobs effectively?

— Do I know how my company stands behind the service it offers and what my duties and the duties of my staff are in the process?

— Do I advertise and sell my company's services outside my working hours?

— Do I support front-line service delivery and back-office service support employees in meeting or exceeding customers' expectations?

— Does my company's advertising create the perception of a superior product or service?

— Do my company's promotional and public relations activities lead to the perception of a superior product or service?

— Do I regularly know how my customers perceive my company's products and services?

— Do I regularly know how my company's employees perceive my company's products and services?

— Do the surroundings in which my company's products and services are delivered contribute to an image and impression of a superior product and service in the minds of customers and employees?

— Do I engage myself and other employees of my company in external activities (conferences, seminars, press conferences, awards, etc.) that add to my company's overall image of superior products and services?

— Do I represent the company and its products and services well in every contact with customers, employees and the general public?

Reflections

— Do I know the reasons why customers are dissatisfied with the service my company provides? Do I know how much it would cost to correct each of the major sources of dissatisfaction?

— Do I know exactly how many customers are dissatisfied with the service my company provides and how much it would cost to handle this dissatisfaction?

— Do I know exactly how many of my dissatisfied customers switch to using competitors and how much profit the company will lose because of this?

— Do I believe in the company I work for, its products and the service being given to customers?

— Do my company's organizational structure and approaches promote the development of conceptual skills in employees at all levels?

— Do I know what my company's service strategy is — exactly? Do my people?

— How often do I contribute ideas for service improvement through the channels available to me?

— When I contribute ideas, do I use all sources of information available to make the idea as realistic to execute as possible?

— Do I actively volunteer for projects, assignments and positions that will allow me to contribute and help me develop new skills?

— For each decision I make or each customer contact I have, do I try to consider how it fits with the company's overall goals, directions and service strategy?

— Does my company's service strategy clearly spell out the importance of satisfying customers? Is the service strategy known at all levels of the organization?

Reflections

— Do performance standards in my company gear performance to deliver service as a number one priority? Do they inspire exceptional satisfaction?

— Do I manage and lead my staff in the way that, down the line, I would like to see my company's customers treated?

— Do my team and I pay attention to actual service delivery? Do we know at all times what the company's service levels are?

— Do my team and I support our company's customer satisfaction tracking systems and encourage customers to respond to them?

— Do my team and I participate fully in any self-audits that are needed?

— Do I regularly schedule myself for visible management assignments — using them for evaluation and paying attention to actual service delivery?

— Do I read and study quality assurance reports, audit reports and customer service reports about my areas of responsibility? Do I take immediate action to solve problems and improve service?

— Am I able to discuss customer satisfaction and actual service delivery in numeric terms with financial impact?

Reflections

3 CUSTOMER EXPECTATIONS

"Customer expectations are at an all-time high — and continue to rise. Most workers are task focused; most managers are profit focused. Who's left to be customer focused?"

Paul Levesque, *The Wow Factory*

Providing good service is not enough. In order for a transaction to be successful, the customer must perceive that he is receiving good service. Customers come to you because they have a need. Determining what that need is, and then meeting it according to their expectations, gets you their business. Keeping that customer happy is what maintains the business.

In this chapter, we will examine how to evaluate a customer's expectations, ways to meet or exceed them, and what it takes to keep that customer coming back — and away from the competition.

Creating Customer Satisfaction

Customer expectations can pose a major challenge because expectations can grow and shrink, as well as change shape and direction. They constantly shift. How satisfied — or not — your customers are is determined by these expectations and your ability to meet or exceed them.

$$\text{Customer satisfaction} = \frac{\text{Your performance}}{\text{Customer expectations}}$$

Your customers' level of satisfaction can be affected by changes in either their expectations or your performance. That means you must pay careful attention to both.

How you perceive your performance may differ significantly from your customers' perceptions. In fact, these discrepancies are not at all unusual. So even if you're working yourself to the bone, if the customer views you as unresponsive — you are unresponsive. Customer satisfaction is driven by their perceptions, not yours. Their perceptions are their reality, and your challenge.

If your customers' satisfaction level is changing, find out what has happened to affect their expectations or perceptions. Whether the change in satisfaction level is positive or negative, find out what is happening. If satisfaction is increasing, determine what you're doing right — and keep it up! If satisfaction is dissipating, figure out how to reverse the situation before it's too late.

Be careful you don't get so involved in delivering services that you lose sight of the customers' expectations and how well they think you're meeting them. Be conscientious in observing what's going on in your customers' environment and your own that could affect their satisfaction level.

> Exceed the customer's expectations every step of the way.
>
> Make the customer feel important.
>
> Tailor the experience to fit the customer.

Look at the Big Picture

Customers are concerned with finding solutions to their problems. Because of this, they have a much broader view of your company than you do. Your view is probably fairly limited to what happens in your department. As a result, your view of the company and your customer's view can sometimes be in conflict.

In order to serve your customers' needs adequately, it's important for you to guard against tunnel vision. Get to know your organization — the entire organization. This is the only way you can truly help your customers achieve their goals. The best way to learn about the organization is to visit other departments and talk with your fellow employees. Learn what they do and what their jobs entail. This information will be useful when you have to interact with them to get a customer's problem solved.

Let's look at an example. Say you are a bank teller. A customer brings you a check for $100 and wants to cash it. You check your records and discover he has only $50 in his account. You explain that you are unable to cash the check because there are insufficient funds to cover it. The customer, on the other hand, claims to have deposited $1000 in the account the day before and demands to know where it is.

Technically, you have done your job. But, just telling the customer that he can't have the money is not helping him find a solution to his problem. Your main concern should be to help the customer find out what happened to his $1000 deposit. If you are familiar with other departments in the bank, you can check on the status of the deposit quickly. And, rather than frustrating the customer, you can provide him with specific answers.

If you need to, call on your supervisor for guidance in these situations. But, be careful not to completely turn the problem over to him. You will be much better off if you use your supervisor strictly as a resource person and follow through on your own. If you do, you will gain the respect of the customer and save your supervisor time.

What Do Customers Want, Anyway?

If you want to keep their business, give customers exactly what they ask for, or even more, without any hesitation. If you do anything less, you might as well offer them nothing, because you'll have lost their good will.

Before you read any further, close the book and write down five or six qualities you think your customers want. Then, reopen the book and continue

23

reading. See how your perspective of what customers want matches what studies have shown they are looking for.

Overall, customers want to be treated fairly, courteously and professionally. Here are some other essential qualities they look for during a service experience:

- **Courtesy.** This sounds basic, but many customers have been lost due to rude service people. As an individual involved in customer contact, it's important for you to leave your problems and your bad moods at the door. Bringing them to work only creates more problems. When a customer walks into your store or calls you on the telephone, he wants to feel welcome. For your part, this involves greeting him enthusiastically, making him feel important and being helpful.

- **Prompt attention.** Nobody likes to wait or feel as though they are being ignored. How many times have you waited at a checkout counter and begun to wonder if anyone was going to take your money? If a customer is left "cooling his heels" while the customer service employee chats with co-workers or attends to other non-customer related details, the customer feels unimportant. If you are busy when a customer walks up, simply look up, smile and say, "I'll be with you in just a minute."

- **Reliability.** Customers want their shopping experience to be as hassle-free as possible. They want to know that when they walk into your store or company, they will find what they want or get an answer to their question. They also expect that, if you make a promise, you will keep it. The greatest source of customer dissatisfaction is broken promises and unmet deadlines. The most important thing to a customer is: Did you do what you promised? Keeping your word is worth more than all the empathy, smiles and chocolates on your pillow in the world. Always underpromise and overdeliver.

- **Personal Attention.** No one likes to feel like a number. And, with today's technology, that can sometimes be a problem. Remember the last time you received a letter in the mail which was obviously a copy and addressed, "Dear Friend"? Chances are you didn't even read it. But, when was the last time you threw out a letter that was obviously an original and began, "Dear Mr. Smith," or "Dear Tom"?

We all like personal attention. It makes us feel important and that makes us feel good. As a customer service employee, you can show customers personal attention by addressing them by their name and by discussing what they need.

- **Responsiveness.** Customers like to feel as though their business is appreciated. And, that's exactly what a customer service employee tells customers when he responds to their needs enthusiastically. If a customer is ignored, he feels as though his business is not appreciated, and he will take it elsewhere where he is met with immediate attention.

- **Knowledgeable staff.** Customers expect customer service employees to be knowledgeable about the products they are selling. In today's high technology and deregulated industries, customers must rely on service employees to help them make choices. For example, a customer calling a travel agent relies heavily on the agent's knowledge to ensure that he is getting the best price on an airline ticket. Nothing sends a customer away like ignorance on the part of the customer service employee.

- **Empathy.** Customers want to be understood. This is particularly true when there is a problem. If the customer service employee acts as though he couldn't care less, the customer will leave feeling that the company doesn't care about its customers. When a customer explains a problem he is having, respond by saying, "I understand why you might feel that way … "

When I'm a Customer, I want:

- Competent, efficient service

- Basic courtesies

- Honesty

- Follow-through

- Not to be bounced around

- Feedback

- Respect

- To be taken seriously

- Knowledgeable help

- Anticipation of my needs

- Friendliness

- To be kept informed

- To be listened to — and heard

- Empathy

- Dedicated attention

- Professional service

- Easy-to-understand explanations

- To be informed of options

Keeping Customers Happy

"For every three people willing to tell a positive story about an experience with your company, there are 33 others who will tell a horror story."

Jerry R. Wilson, Word of Mouth Marketing

Research shows that businesses spend five times as much to attract a new customer as they do to keep a satisfied customer. Also shown is that each year, 65 percent of a company's business will come from repeat customers. From these figures, you can see that keeping customers happy is an important part of your job as a customer service employee. But, how do you do that? Try these six ideas:

1. Act with courtesy

2. Make the customer's experience easy

3. Quickly and efficiently handle mistakes

4. Bend or modify the rules when necessary

5. Know what customers really want

6. Do the job right the first time

Courtesy

Be courteous at all times. Greet the customer with a smile and, if possible, use his name. Everyone likes to hear their name. Courtesy pays off in several ways. It:

- **Encourages repeat business.** Customers like to shop where they feel they are appreciated and comfortable.

- **Promotes future business.** Word-of-mouth is the most credible and least expensive form of advertising. Customers who are treated courteously will tell their friends about the good experience they had. In fact, according to a recent study, word-of-mouth advertising on a consumer's repurchase decision is twice as important as corporate advertising.

- **Eliminates interruptions and distractions.** If you are courteous to your customers they will trust you. As a result, you are less likely to have them call to reconfirm a delivery date or double-check their order.

- **Reduces stress.** If you are courteous to your customers, they will be courteous to you. As a result, you will feel good about the job you are doing and be under less stress.

Making the Customer's Experience Easy

Customers like to shop where it's easy. Nobody likes to go into a store and be ignored or deal with a service employee who is not helpful. When a customer walks into a store looking for help and can't find any, chances are he is going to turn around and walk out. For every customer who walks out, the store loses money and you, in turn, lose a little bit of your job security.

Here are some tips on ways to make a customer's experience with your company easy.

- **Greet the customer warmly.** Walk up to him with a smile and say, "Good morning," "Good afternoon" or "Good evening." Be sure to make eye contact. Make everyone feel welcome.

- **Shake hands.** Shaking hands is viewed as a friendly, professional gesture.

- **Find out the customer's name.** If you don't know the customer's name, tell him yours. Most people will then, in turn, tell you theirs. If you don't catch the name or you're looking at a document with the customer's name and you're not sure how to pronounce it, be sure to ask. Mispronouncing his name will only annoy him.

- **Give the customer the opportunity to express his needs/wants.**

- **Don't get distracted.** Give the customer your undivided attention. Don't allow yourself to be distracted by another employee or something else going on around you. Don't try to do two things at once (talk to a customer and fill out a report, for instance).

- **Treat the customer's request as unique.** This may be the hundredth time today someone has requested this specific item from you, but it is the first for the customer. Treat it as such.

- **Show the customer the value in what you offer.** Be helpful. Anticipate questions or concerns and be ready to address them.

- **Never, never charge more than your estimate.** Build in a cushion just in case. And if you're costs are lower than anticipated, pass the savings on to the customer!

- **The moment a customer asks "Can you … ," your answer should be yes,** even if you can't immediately figure out how. If the customer's request is in any way related to your business, be sure your answer is always "yes!"

Making a customer's experience easy and enjoyable is the best way to keep him coming back. Having him come back costs your company much less than attracting new customers.

When You Make a Mistake

Everyone makes mistakes. But, it's the truly mature, professional person who readily admits it. If you make a mistake, you will probably get much further with the customer if you do the following:

- **Accept responsibility.** Even though the customer may be irritated, he will appreciate your honesty. Be direct. Simply say, "I'm sorry your order is not in. It's my fault. I forgot to process it." Your apology may not eliminate the customer's anger and frustration right away, but it will diminish it. Follow your apology with a demonstration of your desire to correct the problem. Say, "I want to do everything I can to correct the problem. What would be a satisfactory solution?"

- **Don't make excuses.** The customer isn't interested in hearing why you made the mistake. His only concern is getting the problem resolved satisfactorily.

- **Negotiate a solution.** Once you've apologized and accepted responsibility, you need to get right on to the business at hand — correcting the mistake. Tell the customer how you intend to correct the problem and see if that's satisfactory. If not, you may have to negotiate.

- **Don't avoid telling the customer.** Tell the customer as soon as you realize you made a mistake. You can turn a problem into an opportunity if you catch the mistake before the customer does and call him to apologize and propose a remedy. While the customer may be unhappy to hear about the problem, he will also appreciate your diligence in catching the mistake and your commitment to correcting it.

When Rules and Regulations Get in the Way

Companies have to have rules and regulations for consistency's sake. But, when taken to extremes, rules and regulations can tie the hands of the customer service employee and make it difficult for him to do his job.

Although rules should not be broken, they should be flexible. Unfortunately, in many companies, customer service employees aren't given the authority to bend rules when necessary.

Review the rules and regulations in your company. Make sure you understand why they exist and if there are exceptions to any of the rules. In order to explain them to customers, you need to understand the thinking behind the rules.

Find out if your company allows you to use your discretion when it comes to the rules and exactly how much flexibility you have. Being able to handle a customer's problem, or potential problem, on the spot is sometimes more important than enforcing a rule to the letter.

Take the case of the gentleman who arrived at a hotel at the designated 3 o'clock check-in time only to discover that his room was not ready. Looking irritated, he told the desk clerk about how his day had gone. He had missed his first flight and then his second flight had been canceled. Due to all the confusion, he had not eaten lunch.

The desk clerk took the initiative and invited him to go into the hotel's dining room and have lunch at the hotel's expense, even though this was not standard procedure. The man did, and by the time he returned, his room was ready and he was in a much better frame of mind.

Stay as flexible as possible while staying within the rules. If you find that a particular rule or procedure causes chronic problems, first document the problems it causes, then talk to your supervisor to see if a change can be made.

Knowing What Customers Really Want

Don't guess about what your customers want. They're more than willing to tell you. Make it easy for them. Create a short questionnaire — three to five questions is usually sufficient. If they don't want to respond, fine. Don't pester them. But if you routinely ask for feedback and don't get it, ask yourself these questions:

- Do I ask enough questions?

- Do I ask the right questions?

- Do I communicate effectively about why I am asking the questions?

- Do I ask the right people?

- Do I know how to use the data I collect?

- Am I organized to respond to the information?

- Do I value and trust the information I receive?

No one likes to hear they've done a lousy job, but criticism from customers is more valuable than praise. You want your customers to tell you when you've messed up, so that you can take care of the problem and ensure it doesn't happen again — to them or anyone else. If they don't tell you, they'll walk away shaking their heads and they'll never come back. Even worse, you're likely to alienate someone else in the future by doing exactly the same thing. Your goal is to create a feedback relationship designed to prevent problems from occurring in the first place.

Do the Job Right the First Time

Being nice to people is just 20 percent of providing good customer service. The important part is designing systems that allow you to do the job right the first time. All the smiles in the world aren't going to help you if your product or service is not what the customer wants.

- What is the benefit to the customer?

- Will the customer easily understand that benefit?

- What impact will this idea, program or system have on our employees?

- How will it affect our existing systems?

- Is anybody else doing it successfully? What can we learn from their experience?

- What could go wrong?

- Will it give us an advantage over our competitors?

- How much will it cost?

- Will it make money?

- When should we evaluate it?

Ten Tips to Keep Your Customers Coming Back

1. Do what you say — and more. Underpromise and overdeliver.

2. Follow up with new customers personally. Make sure the product is delivered as promised and performs as expected.

3. Empower front-line people to do whatever is necessary to satisfy an unhappy customer on the spot.

4. Identify all selling opportunities — and train, train, and then train some more.

5. Survey customers to discover their unfulfilled expectations and undisclosed needs ... then fill them.

6. Do something special to reward repeat customers.

7. Secretly shop your own organization. Do you feel welcome, comfortable and understood?

8. Reward your people for exceptional service.

9. Track response time in resolving customer complaints — then shorten it.

10. Make each and every employee feel unique, special and appreciated. They'll pass those feelings on to your customers.

Conclusion

Keeping customers happy is imperative if you want them to come back. This can be achieved by displaying common courtesy, making the experience easy and meeting the customers' needs. Do the job right the first time and encourage feedback about your weaknesses or errors.

As you work with customers, think about how you like to be treated. This will help you provide what others expect.

In determining what customers are looking for, try to view the experience through their eyes. How would you want to be treated? What would you expect? Use your own experiences to help you create the kind of atmosphere that makes a customer want to come back.

Who are your customers (by category)?

What unique expectations of you does each group have?

What could you do to exceed each unique expectation?

What could you do to ensure each customer knows this is being done with them in mind?

What are the steps your customers typically go through to do business with you?

What could you do at each step to exceed the customers' expectations?

What could you do at each step to make the customer feel important?

Reflections

4 EFFECTIVE COMMUNICATION

Communication is fundamental to your job as a customer service employee. In fact, it has been estimated that more than half of your job consists of communication. In order to be effective, you have to communicate with customers, co-workers, other departments and sometimes vendors outside your company. As we discussed earlier, it doesn't matter how good a job you do, the important thing is how the customer perceives the job you are doing.

Communication is a two-way sharing of information that results in an understanding between the receiver and the sender. If both don't have the same understanding of the message, they are not truly communicating. Communication is the key to how you are perceived.

In this chapter, we will address how to make your communication skills work well for you in your pursuit of customer service excellence.

Communication Breakdowns

Communication between two people can break down when emotions, attitudes, nonverbal clues, role expectations or the wrong choice of words get in the way.

- **Emotions.** Strong emotions can sometimes cause a listener to tune out. For example, if a customer comes to you and says, "You did this all wrong," your first response may be to become defensive. If you are concentrating on defending yourself instead of encouraging the customer to explain what the problem is, you won't come any closer to solving the problem.

- **Attitude.** Attitudes are expressed by the way you act, look and demonstrate feelings. If you convey a negative attitude, it affects what the other person hears. For example, if you adopt a superior attitude, the listener is going to concentrate on your air of superiority and not hear what you are actually saying. If your response on the above example was, "Well dear, here's the problem. It's obvious ... ," the individual will probably be so intent on the superior, sarcastic attitude you are conveying that she won't even hear your response.

- **Nonverbal clues.** How you stand, how you dress and especially the expression on your face all affect how you communicate. For example, if you work in a jewelry store and come dressed in jeans and a T-shirt, your customers will probably not take you seriously. They will be so busy looking at the way you're dressed, they won't hear all the wonderful things you say about the diamond ring in your hand — no matter how knowledgeable you are. Your appearance can also devalue the quality of the merchandise in the eyes of the customer.

  Be particularly careful with your facial expressions. A raised eyebrow, pursed lips or general look of annoyance or irritation may disrupt an otherwise smooth conversation with a customer.

- **Role expectations.** This involves how others expect you to act. If you do not come across in the manner they anticipate, they may become distracted, thus breaking down communication. If you are introduced by a fellow employee as an expert in widgets, and then you can't answer their simplest questions, they are going to find it difficult to communicate with you. This type of communication problem can also create a negative impression of the company you work for, as well as the products or services you offer.

- **Choice of words.** The words you choose to communicate your message can sometimes cause a communications breakdown. Choose your words carefully. Let's look at an example of how words can make a difference.

Customer: "I would like to get a refund."

Customer Service: "We can't refund your money for that merchandise. If you didn't want it, you should have returned it within 30 days like our policy states."

There are several things wrong with the above response. First, the employee uses negative phrases which are bound to put the customer on the defensive: "can't," "didn't want" and "should have."

Second, she says, "If you didn't want it … " Does she know for a fact that the customer didn't want it or is she making an assumption? Finally, she throws the policy manual in the customer's face without even knowing if the customer was made aware of the policy.

A much more effective way to handle the situation would be to say,

"May I ask why you are returning this merchandise? Let me tell you what I can do. I can give you a voucher in the amount of the purchase, which you can use to buy anything else in the store. Let's take care of that right now."

Verbal Communication

When you talk to a customer you express yourself both verbally and non-verbally. Both can have an impact on your message. Here are some tips on making the most of your verbal communication.

- **Greet the customer warmly.** Extend your hand and wear a smile. This will make the customer feel welcome and get your transaction off to a good start.

- **Be precise.** Don't use phrases like, "I'll do my best." The customer has no idea what "your best" is. If you're dealing with a problem, she may think that your best is getting the problem resolved, when actually your best may only be finding out why the mistake happened.

- **Don't leave out any details.** If you tell a customer that a product costs $20, that is what she is going to expect. If there are additional charges, be sure and let her know up front. For example, the product may cost $20, but if there is an additional $2 charge for taxes and a $5 charge for shipping, and she doesn't know it, then she will be upset.

- **Think before you speak.** The more you know about the customer, the better you can serve her. If you think about what you're going to say before you start talking, you'll be better able to get your message across.

- **Use small talk sparingly.** It's okay to engage in a little small talk to break the ice, but don't let it distract you from your original goal: to help the customer find what she needs.

Nonverbal Communication

Nonverbal messages affect the way you communicate. In fact, experts say that nonverbal communication accounts for half of what we communicate. Tone of voice accounts for 40 percent and the actual words only 10 percent. So, you can see how important nonverbal messages are in communication.

What are nonverbal messages? Anything you do that distracts or enhances what you are saying. Your smile, posture, dress and gestures are all examples of nonverbal communication. They can work for you or against you.

For example, if you dress professionally, customers will be more apt to think of you, and treat you, as a professional. They will give credence to what you say even before you open your mouth.

If you slouch, customers will interpret it as a lack of self-confidence and presume you are not knowledgeable about the product, even though you may know it backward and forward. Think about the nonverbal clues you give. Are you saying, "Hi, I'm a knowledgeable professional, and I want to help you," or are you giving the impression that you are indifferent to your job and the customer?

Evaluate your nonverbal messages carefully and make sure you're projecting the image you want to get across.

Listening

Another important part of communicating is listening. Listening involves more than what you hear with your ears. It involves what you hear with your mind. You may hear the words, but unless you really listen to what is being said, you won't be able to respond to the customer's request.

Many people have a hard time listening because they allow themselves to be distracted. If you can break yourself of that habit, you will become a much better listener. Becoming distracted when someone is speaking is easy. Studies show that the average person speaks at a rate of approximately 125 words per minute. However, we have the ability to process what we hear at the rate of more than 500 words a minute. The result is that sometimes the brain gets bored and wanders to other things. We've all experienced it. You are sitting in a crowded auditorium listening to a speech. The next thing you know everybody is clapping, and you suddenly realize that you don't know what the speaker said. (You may, however, have your entire dinner menu planned out in your mind.)

Are you a good listener? Before you answer too quickly, ask yourself these four questions:

- When someone else is talking, do I sometimes interrupt?

- When someone else is talking, do I sometimes finish sentences for them?

- When someone else is talking, am I sometimes thinking about what I'm going to say next instead of what that person is saying now?

- When I meet a new person, do I think I've learned that person's name only to discover in a few minutes that I am clueless?

These are four red flags that signal we have some work to do on our listening skills. Try the following techniques.

Listen for facts and feelings. People express themselves with both facts ("The tape recorder that I bought from you broke during a major interview") and feelings ("I'm very upset because I missed my deadline"). What this person is doing is stating the fact that the tape recorder is broken and expressing her feelings of anger and disappointment. In developing a response, you have to address both. Your response to this situation might be, "I'm sorry this happened. I'm sure it caused you some anxiety and inconvenience. Let me get you a new one, and let's test it to make sure it works before you leave the store."

Become actively involved in the conversation. Don't just sit back and listen without any kind of response. If you understand what the individual is saying, let her know by nodding your head or by saying, "Yes, I understand." If you don't understand, stop her and ask for clarification.

Don't be distracted. Don't let other employees, customers or things going on around you steal your attention. If you're not giving the customer your total attention, you're bound to miss an important point. Customers can tell when you're distracted, and the message it conveys to them is that they and their problems or concerns are not important to you.

Wait until the customer finishes talking before formulating your response. It's human nature to want to respond immediately. But often, we start thinking about what we're going to say or do before the individual finishes talking. Avoid answering too quickly. Make sure you don't miss anything the customer says. If you don't wait, you may miss out on important information that you need to respond to effectively.

Don't prejudge. Don't let a customer's appearance or manner distract you from what she has to say. If you look at an individual and decide that she can't afford your top-of-the-line product because of the way she is dressed, you may be missing out on an important sale. Looks can be deceiving. Consider the woman who went into a luxury car dealership dressed in the clothes she works in around the house. One salesperson sized her up quickly and concluded she couldn't afford one of the cars. Another salesperson, however, decided to practice her selling skills and approached the woman. Not only did she buy a car for herself, but she later returned and bought one for her mother.

Clarify what's been said. Once the customer finishes telling you what she wants, restate her request to ensure that you fully understand. In doing so, be sure to use "I" statements. Say, "As I understand it, you would like the biggest widget we have," rather than, "You said you want the biggest widget we have." If that's not what the customer said, she will be irritated if she thinks she has been misquoted.

Listening is imperative for proper communication. If customers feel they are not being listened to, they will begin to speak louder and become more emphatic. This can cause embarrassment and result in an unpleasant experience for both of you. Retain control of the situation at all times.

In communicating with the customer, find out what she really wants. Don't let her get by with making vague statements such as, "I want to return this because it doesn't work." Saying it doesn't work may mean:

- It is broken and doesn't work.

- She doesn't know how to use it and can't get it to work.

- It doesn't fit her needs, and so it doesn't work for her in the specific application she had hoped it would.

- It doesn't work the way she thought it would.

Your response would be different in each scenario. It's up to you to probe and ask questions that will lead you to the real problem, which allows you to effectively correct it.

The Art of Questioning

Part of helping the customer get what she wants involves defining her exact needs. You have to listen to not only what the customer says, but also what she doesn't say. Sometimes customers have a hard time expressing themselves. When this happens, you have to get to the real issue by probing. As a customer service employee, you do this through questioning.

There are two basic types of questions you can ask: open and closed. Open questions are used as a springboard for discussion. Closed are used when all you want, or need, are yes-and-no answers. Using both types of questions helps you gain control of the conversation.

Use open questions to:

- Define problems

- Establish needs

- Understand requests

- Get more information

Use closed questions to:

- Get the customer to agree

- Clarify what has been said

- Summarize a conversation

- Confirm an order

Communicating by Phone

When customers call on the telephone, you don't have the advantage of being able to read their nonverbal clues. Therefore, answering questions or solving problems over the phone involves different skills.

Just like face-to-face contact, the way you greet the customer will set the tone for the conversation that follows. When answering phone calls, follow these four basic rules:

- Greet the caller

- Give the name of your organization or department

- State your name

- Offer assistance

For example, "Good morning. This is John Smith in customer service. How may I help you?"

Be enthusiastic and smile even before you pick up the receiver. Callers may not be able to see your smile, but they will hear it.

Listen carefully to what the callers say. Most of the time, they will be calling to:

- Make a statement

- Voice an objection

- Ask a question

If a customer voices an objection, address it immediately. Don't ignore it. For example, if the customer says, "I tried to buy the light bulbs that were on sale, and there weren't any left. I don't think you ever did have any of the advertised specials." Respond to the objection before you solve the problem. If the customer is correct and the store did not have the specials, explain why.

"You're right, Ms. Smith, we didn't have the light bulbs. When we placed our ad, the shipment was scheduled to arrive in time for the sale. Unfortunately, a snowstorm detained it. I will be happy to send you a rain check so you can get the light bulbs at the advertised price. I will also send you a post card and let you know when the light bulbs are in stock."

Be careful not to confuse a statement and an objection. If you do, you may get sidetracked trying to counter the objection and lose control of the conversation. For example, a customer may say, "The claims your product makes are unbelievable." Depending on how she says it, she may mean the claims are false, the product doesn't work as promised, or that the claims are exciting. If you begin to defend the product, you may never find out why she actually called. If you have any doubts about what the customer is saying, ask an open-ended question to get more information. For instance, "Unbelievable? In what way?"

Here are some tips for dealing effectively with customers on the phone.

- Make sure you understand all the features of your phone. Nothing is more irritating than to be put on hold and suddenly hear a dial tone. If you're uncertain how to use the features, ask your supervisor or a fellow employee to explain them before you get a customer on the line.

- Answer the phone as quickly as possible. The standard rule of thumb in a business is to answer the phone within three rings. Customers will develop an impression of you and your company by the number of times they have to listen to the phone ring.

- Hold the mouthpiece directly in front of your mouth and speak clearly. If the mouthpiece is off to the side, your comments will sound garbled. Speak clearly and in an audible tone. Avoid making the customer strain in order to hear you.

- Avoid unnecessary noise. Don't wear jewelry that is constantly banging into the phone, have a radio on nearby, or shuffle papers. It is very distracting to the caller.

- Don't talk with others while on a call. If you do, the customer will feel like you are not giving her request or problem your full attention. You won't be able to respond appropriately because you won't know what has been said.

- Don't eat, drink or chew gum while talking on the phone. This is not only distracting, but also rude.

- Always use the hold button when you ask a customer to wait. Don't just put the receiver down. Can you imagine how embarrassing it would be if an unsuspecting co-worker started talking about a subject not meant for the customer's ears, and it was overheard by the customer on the other end of the line?

- Ask permission to place the caller on hold. Don't say, "Hold please," and immediately depress the hold button. Ask if it is okay with the customer, and then wait for a response. Saying, "The other line is ringing, may I put you on hold for just a minute," is a much nicer way of handling the situation.

- Don't leave a customer hanging on hold. If you must put a customer on hold, don't leave her there for an inappropriate amount of time. It is common business practice not to leave a customer on hold any longer than one minute. If you can't find the information you need or get an answer to her question in that amount of time, ask for a phone number and tell her you will call back, giving the approximate time. "I can have an answer for you within 10 minutes," or "I can get back to you later this afternoon," makes the customer feel more in control of the situation.

Using Excellent Telephone Skills

1. Practice basic telephone answering etiquette

2. Plan your call

3. Listen with care; get the facts and the emotions

4. Tie up all loose ends before ending the call

5. Transfer politely

6. Use voice mail effectively

7. Use the hold button as little as possible — and with style when it is necessary to use it at all

---

When You Have to Say No

Unfortunately, you won't always be able to do what the customer wants. You can, however, make the experience less frustrating for her if you follow a few simple rules:

- Explain why it can't be done. Don't just say you can't do it. Give details. Explain why you can't do what the customer has requested.

- Don't quote policy — tell the underlying reasons why. For example, don't say, "Our policy won't allow me to refund your money without a receipt." Instead say, "I can't refund your money for this sweater because our winter merchandise has all been sold. Therefore, we can't put it back on the rack."

- Don't patronize. There is nothing more frustrating to a customer than being talked down to. Keep your comments on a professional, adult level.

- Offer alternatives. Don't just say no, try to help the customer find a solution to her problem. Using the example above, you might say, "I can't refund your money. However, I can give you a credit voucher which you can use to buy other merchandise in the store."

- Concentrate on the positives. Don't dwell on the negatives. For example, instead of saying, "I can't help you," say, "Here is what I can do." This approach will convince the customer that you are trying to help her.

Express Yourself

Sometimes it's not what you say, but how you say it. Review these sample statements to determine ways to improve how you say what you say.

- Avoid making excuses. Saying, "I'm sorry, but as you can see we are pretty backlogged," isn't going to impress the customer. She will probably feel that you didn't think her order was important enough to give it priority. Instead say, "I'm sorry your order hasn't been processed yet. Let me see what happened." This personalizes the response and lets the customer know that you will try to find a solution.

- Eliminate phrases such as, "you will have to." Command statements such as these tend to make the customer defensive and give her the feeling that she is being put off. Instead of saying, "I can't help you with that. You'll have to talk to someone in our shipping department," you might say something like, "May I transfer you to our shipping department? They will be able to trace your shipment and tell you when you can expect it." This helps the customer feel like she is in control.

- Don't point the finger at other employees. Making such accusations makes you look less than professional and gives the customer the feeling that the people within your company don't work well together. It also makes her wonder whether or not she will get her problem resolved. A better way to state it would be, "According to my records, you should have received your order by now. Let me call our shipping department to see if there is a reason why it hasn't arrived." This makes the customer feel like you work with others in your company to get problems resolved quickly.

- Avoid making nonspecific statements. Customers who are told that the salespeople "will try" or "will do their best" may become suspicious of just how hard they'll try. The customer may believe that what the customer service employee is actually saying is that she will go through the motions, but won't necessarily make a sincere effort on the part of the customer.

- Don't give unnecessary details. The customer doesn't need to know that Mr. Smith can't help her because he is at the doctor. Simply say, "Mr. Smith is not in right now. May I have him call you, or can I help you?" Also avoid statements like, "I don't know where Mr. Smith is. I guess he is still out to lunch." These kinds of statements make Mr. Smith look irresponsible and your entire company look bad.

- Avoid the phrase, "should be." Don't tell a customer that the technician "should be there within an hour," unless you are certain that she will arrive by then. The customer will expect her to be there. If the technician doesn't arrive within an hour, the customer will be upset with you for leading her on, and upset with the technician for not showing up when she was "supposed to."

- Don't mention other complaints. Avoiding making statements like, "He can't help you right now. He is handling another complaint," or "I'm sure we can do something. Another customer had the same problem last week." These kinds of statements lead the customer to believe that your company has a lot of complaints, and that's not the message you want to convey.

Conclusion

Communication is an important part of your job. If you do it effectively, you create loyal customers. If you don't, you will look bad and so will your company.

Effective communication involves both speaking and listening skills. It is not something you are born knowing how to do. They are skills you have to acquire through practice. Learn them and they will serve you well.

General Communication

Think about the people you deal with regularly. What are their communication strengths? Weaknesses?

What would they identify as your communication strengths and weaknesses?

Outline a plan to improve upon your areas of weakness and further sharpen your strengths.

Telephone Communication (answer each question)

Do you answer the phone with a positive tone of voice and a smile?

How quickly do you answer? One ring? Two?

Are you frequently asked to repeat yourself?

Do you transfer calls by first bringing on-line the third party and determining she is the correct person to take the call?

Do you explain to the third party what the customer needs ... or do you make the customer explain it all again?

Are you a good listener?

Do you take notes?

Do you leave a time of return on your outgoing voice-mail message?

Do you repeat numbers and names when leaving messages?

Do you ask permission — and really mean it — before putting someone on hold?

Reflections

5 HANDLING DIFFICULT OR SPECIAL CUSTOMERS

Basically, all customers want the same thing — good service. But every once in a while, you will come across a customer who requires special treatment. Knowing how to handle these individuals will help make your job a little easier. This chapter is devoted to tips for dealing with special cases.

The Angry Customer

When angry customers call or come into your store or company, they have two messages they want to deliver: one has to do with facts, and the other has to do with their feelings. It's up to you to get past the feelings so you can get the facts you need to solve their problems.

In dealing with an angry customer, don't deny his anger. Telling a customer, "There's really no reason to get upset," is only going to make him angrier.

Here are some ways you can defuse an angry customer.

- **Keep your own emotions in check.** Don't allow yourself to lose control. Determine the overall objective of the complaint (i.e., getting the customer a refund, finding the product he is looking for) and concentrate on it, not the customer's angry words. Returning the customer's anger with like responses will only escalate the situation even further.

- **Don't allow yourself to get defensive.** When you get defensive, it means you are becoming emotionally involved, as if the customer were attacking you personally. It's not personal. Stay objective and emotionally detached.

- **Look beyond the anger.** Often what you are seeing is the individual's frustration that is brought upon by unrelated problems. His anger may not have anything to do with the problem he is experiencing with your company. It may involve external factors such as personal problems, a flat tire or an argument with his boss. If you remember there are often other forces at work, you will deal more effectively with an angry customer.

- **Anticipate potentially volatile situations.** Most of the time you can anticipate some of the things that are likely to make a customer angry. If possible, avoid these situations. For example, telling a customer, "There is nothing I can do," will generally upset him. Take a positive approach and say, "Let me see what I can do."

- **Customers get annoyed when they are shuffled between departments,** whether they are on the phone or standing in your store or office. Make every attempt to handle the problem yourself. If you can't, explain what needs to be done, who the customer needs to talk to, etc. Help make the process as easy as possible for the customer (help him fill out forms or personally take him to another office or department).

  If the customer is on the telephone, take his name and number before you transfer him. Also, tell him who he will be talking with. Stay on the line, if possible, until the transfer has been made.

- **Defuse the anger.** Let the customer get it all off his chest. He needs to vent. Eventually he will run out of steam. Until he does, however, nothing you can say will have any impact on him. Because of his highly emotional state, the logic of your responses or explanations will simply not register with him ... and may even make him more volatile. Wait him out, then try to find things the two of you can agree on. This will help you find an acceptable solution to the problem.

- **Don't make promises you can't keep.** Don't let a customer get you to make a promise in the heat of the moment that you can't keep. It will only cause you problems in the future.

- **Be sympathetic.** Indifference will send a customer out the door faster than failing to solve the problem. In fact, studies show that 68 percent of customers stop doing business with companies because of indifferent treatment by their employees. This compares to 14 percent who leave because of product dissatisfaction, and 9 percent who leave because of competition. Listen carefully to what the customer has to say and let him know that you understand. For example, you might say, "I understand that this can be very frustrating. Let me see what I can do to help resolve this problem."

  Don't, however, agree with the customer if he begins criticizing the company. This approach will get you nowhere. You will lose the respect of the customer, and if your company finds out what you have said, you may lose your job.

- **Analyze the problem.** When customers are angry, they often don't express the real problem clearly. They are so intent on making sure you understand their anger that they may forget to communicate some vital information that will help you solve the problem. As a customer service employee, it is your responsibility to uncover the exact problem and help the customer find a solution. Ask probing questions and repeat what the customer has said to make sure you understand fully.

- **Stress what you can do, not what you can't.** A response of, "Let me see what I can do to help you," will defuse a customer's anger a lot faster than, "I don't know what we can do about this."

- **Ask the customer how he would like the problem resolved.** If it is within the realm of your authority and it is a reasonable request, do it. If not, negotiate a solution that both the customer and your company will be happy with.

- **Act on the problem.** Acting on the problem involves more than simply saying that you will take care of it. If there are several problems, set priorities and attack the most critical ones first. For example, if you are a travel agent and your customer calls to say that he is stuck in Tanzania because the airline you booked him on has just declared bankruptcy, find him a flight home first, then work on getting a refund.

- **Identify any potential problems that may arise.** If a customer is returning merchandise, for example, and you tell him that a credit will appear on his statement, tell him which statement. The customer may not realize that the closing date on his account has already passed. If the credit doesn't show up on his next statement, he will be calling you back. By explaining when he can expect the credit, you keep the customer happy and reduce the likelihood of getting another angry call.

- **Follow through.** Just because you have found a solution to the problem doesn't mean the problem has been solved. It's up to you to follow through and make certain that what you have promised actually happens. If it doesn't, you are bound to face another confrontation with the customer. For example, if a customer returns a defective item and you promise that credit will be issued on his account, don't just write a request and hope it happens. Call the credit department to make sure this happens.

The Unhappy Customer

We all know them — individuals who walk around with chips on their shoulders. They walk into your store and make a statement such as, "I'm sure you don't have what I'm looking for." They don't necessarily have a problem with you or your company, their problem is with life in general.

You can't expect to change the unhappy customer, but you can make the situation as easy as possible and protect yourself from being dragged into a bad mood.

Show these people as much compassion and warmth as possible. Chances are you won't be able to improve their moods, but you can determine exactly what it is they are looking for and, as a result, help them find it.

The Argumentative Customer

These people thrive on arguments. If you tell them a sweater is white, they'll say it's black. They are aggressive and probably disagree with, or question, everything you say.

Your first instinct is to disagree and argue back. Don't allow yourself to fall into the trap. In dealing with these people, try the following techniques.

- **Speak softly.** If you speak loudly, they will speak louder and louder, and soon you will both be shouting at each other.

- **Ask their opinion.** Argumentative people like to feel they are in control. If you try to rob them of that control, they become more argumentative. If, on the other hand, you give them some control, they are liable to ease up. For example, instead of saying, "This stereo is the best buy," you might tell a customer about all of the options available and the price on a couple of different stereos. Then ask him, "Which do you think is the best buy?"

- **Concentrate on points of agreement.** Look for things you both agree on and build your conversation around them. For example, "You like XYZ's brand of stereo. So do I. I feel they make a very reliable piece of equipment. Don't you agree?"

- **Take five.** If you allow yourself to become angry, excuse yourself briefly and regain your composure. If you don't think you can deal effectively with the customer, ask another customer service employee to take over.

The Talkative Customer

These individuals can eat up a lot of your time if you let them. They come in to buy a widget, and by the time they leave, you know their entire life story. If no other customers are around, it may not be a problem to take the time to listen, but if others are waiting, you need to move the talker along.

Try to keep in mind that the reason most of these people talk so much is because they are lonely. Don't brush them off. Show compassion and interest, but make it clear that you do have to assist other customers.

The Flirt

Flirts can be either men or women. The entire time you are trying to help them, they keep making comments with double meanings and sexual innuendoes. As they do, they watch you carefully to see if you react in any way.

The reaction of most customer service employees is to become embarrassed, defensive or put them down. None of these techniques is particularly effective. The more embarrassed or upset you get, the more comments they make.

In dealing with these customers, remain professional at all times. Ignore their remarks and instead concentrate your efforts on helping them with the product or service they are seeking. After all, the sooner they find what they are looking for, the sooner they will leave.

The Nontalker

It's like trying to pull teeth to get this customer to tell you what he is looking for. It may be because he honestly isn't sure, or it may be because he has a hard time expressing himself.

Be patient. Make him feel relaxed. Don't ask questions that require elaborate answers. For example, you may say something like, "Well, let's look at these two shirts. Between the two, which do you prefer? The blue one? That's my favorite too. It's more tailored, and it will give you a more distinguished look."

By doing this, you have made the customer feel comfortable, assured him that he has good taste and, at the same time, you've gotten some idea about the style and color of shirt he prefers.

His body language will also give you a clue as to what he is thinking. His verbal response may be the same to every shirt you pick out for him, "Yeah," but his face will tell you if you are on the right track.

The Habitual Complainer

The habitual complainer doesn't like anything. The service is poor, the prices are too high ... chances are even the design of the building is probably "all wrong." Don't let this individual discourage you or drag you down. Realize that this is just part of his personality.

When the habitual complainer calls, try to separate legitimate complaints from phony ones. Avoid becoming defensive, regardless of what he says. Let him talk.

If the complaint is legitimate, take the necessary steps to correct it and, like you would with any other customer, apologize for the inconvenience.

One warning! Be careful not to assume that everything the complainer complains about is frivolous. Although he sets himself up for this kind of response by crying wolf, it's up to you as a professional to distinguish between the legitimate and frivolous complaints.

The Obnoxious or Rude Customer

If you realize what these people are really like, it may be easier for you to deal with them. Often, they come across as arrogant and totally self-assured. Underneath, however, they are lonely and insecure.

Your first thought in dealing with obnoxious people may be to become sarcastic or "put them in their place." Don't do it. A much more effective recourse is to be nice — exceptionally nice. They won't know how to handle it, and eventually will begin giving you the same respect that you give them.

The Demanding Customer

These are the individuals who interrupt you when you are in the middle of a conversation with another customer and demand your immediate attention. Once again, this reaction is borne out of a sense of insecurity. By being demanding, they feel more in control.

Treat them with the same respect you would any other customer, but don't give in to their demands. You can do this by concentrating on their needs and not their manner. Their demands are actually their needs. Think of them as such, and you will be able to respond more positively.

The Indecisive Customer

Like the talkative customer, these individuals can eat up a lot of your time — time you should be spending with other customers. These individuals are truly terrified of making the wrong decision. They don't trust their own judgment. In dealing with indecisive customers, try these approaches:

- **Create a relaxing environment.** If you are calm and understanding, you make them feel more confident and, thus, better able to make a decision.

- **Limit the possibilities.** This can be done most effectively by finding out ahead of time exactly what it is they want. For example, if you determine they want a black suit to wear for formal occasions, you can limit the number of suits you show them and, thus, their options.

- **Offer a way out.** Explain the store's return policy. Say, "You know, Mr. Smith, you can return this suit if you decide it's not right for you once you get it home." It will make him less fearful of making a mistake, and chances are, he won't return it. Just knowing he has the option will help him make a decision.

- **Be patient.** If you try to rush these individuals, you're only going to make matters worse. One of their biggest fears is making a snap decision that they'll regret later. Make it clear that they can take all the time they need. Then, if necessary, you can tell them that while they are thinking about their decision, you will help the next customer.

The Abusive Customer

If a customer becomes abusive, remain calm. Keep reminding yourself that he is not angry at you personally, but frustrated by the situation or other problems in his life.

If the customer begins talking loudly, lower your voice. Doing so will force him to listen more carefully. Eventually, he will lower his voice to match yours.

Talk at a normal pace. If you begin to talk quickly, it will only make matters worse. The customer will think that you are nervous, or worse yet, that you only want to get rid of him.

If a customer uses abusive language or makes threats, be direct. Address the customer by name and say, "Mr. Smith, I understand that you are upset, but do not use that language." If a customer threatens you, document the incident and pass it along to your supervisor.

People with Heavy Accents

Sometimes trying to communicate with foreign-born customers who have heavy accents can be difficult. Misunderstandings can result. To help you deal effectively with individuals who have heavy accents, try these techniques:

- **Be patient and concentrate.** Remember, they are just as frustrated as you are. If you are patient and concentrate on the conversation, you will be better able to understand what they are saying.

- **Speak slowly and distinctly.** Don't speak so slowly that it appears to be an insult, but speak slow enough that they can follow what you are saying. Also, if you speak slowly, they will do the same.

- **Be extra courteous.** This shows them that you really do care and want to help. It also helps them relax and eases their frustration.

- **Avoid using slang or industry jargon.** Use plain, simple English. Don't use terms or phrases that will only add to their confusion.

- **Speak in a normal tone.** Don't shout. When someone is having a hard time understanding us, our first reaction is often to speak louder. Speaking louder won't help; in fact, it will probably only cause more anxiety. And, if you speak louder, the customer will begin to speak louder too.

- **Don't try to listen to every word.** Listen carefully for key words and phrases which sum up what the customer is trying to tell you. If you try to catch every word, you will probably miss the overall message.

- **Reiterate what has been said.** Once the customer has told you what the problem is, summarize what he said, stating your response in the form of a question that can be answered yes or no. For example, "You would like to return this dress because it is the wrong size. Am I correct?"

- **Don't ask, "Do you understand?"** This question sounds negative, and the customer may feel that he is being insulted.

- **Avoid humor or wisecracks.** Stick to solving the problem. Different cultures take humor in different ways. You don't want to risk insulting the customer.

- **Write it down.** If you feel that you are truly not communicating verbally, try writing it down. Many times, foreign-born people can read and write English better than they can speak it. Just like with speaking, use simple, short sentences in expressing your thoughts.

- **If you speak another language, try using it.** The individual you are trying to communicate with may understand the other language better than English.

- **Listen to foreign-language tapes.** If you live in an area where there are a lot of people of a particular foreign nationality, pick up some foreign-language tapes and listen to them. It's not necessary to learn the language, but the tapes will help you become familiar with the foreign sounds.

Handling Complicated Problems

If a customer comes to you with a complicated problem, don't rely on your memory to help get it solved. Listen carefully as the customer describes the problem and take notes.

As is the case with handling any problem, reiterate what the customer has told you to make sure that you fully understand. You can say, "If I understand you correctly, this is what happened." This not only ensures that you understand the situation, it also helps the customer determine if he has left out any relevant facts which will help you solve the problem.

Working with Senior Citizens

Senior citizens have more disposable income today than at any other time. To attract this important segment of the population, many companies are offering special senior-citizen incentives.

But, incentives are not enough to win customer loyalty. Like most people, seniors want to be treated fairly and courteously. Here are some general tips to help you deal with senior citizens.

- **Be cordial.** Take the extra time to be especially warm and friendly. Most seniors appreciate this sort of relationship building.

- **Don't shout.** While you should speak slowly and distinctly, there is no need to shout. If you do, the senior may take it as an insult.

- **Don't patronize.** Chances are the person's IQ is the same as yours. If you talk down to him, you will lose him.

- **Be thorough.** Many seniors keep extensive and exact records of transactions. They appreciate it if you do the same.

- **Be patient.** At times, you may feel that a senior is being repetitious or long-winded in explaining his problem. Give him the time he needs to explain his situation thoroughly. Reiterating what he told you will convince him that you understood what he said.

- **Be their advocate.** Seniors, like other customers, get frustrated when they feel they are getting the runaround. You can make them your friend if you act as their advocate and help steer them through the company's policies and procedures to find a solution to their problem.

Conclusion

Serving nice people is easy. Difficult people, however, can be a challenge. If you accept this challenge, you will experience great personal satisfaction and, at the same time, win loyal customers for your company.

Customers, no matter how difficult, are people just like you. Sometimes they allow their moods to get in the way. When that happens, remember, don't take it personally. Realizing that other problems are causing their anger should make it easier for you to deal effectively with them.

1. Which types of customers do you deal with most often? Rank these 13 types in order of the frequency with which you are faced with these special situations.

   Angry

   Unhappy

   Argumentative

   Talkative

   Flirt

   Nontalker

   Habitual Complainer

   Obnoxious/Rude

   Demanding

   Indecisive

   Abusive

   Heavy Accents

   Senior Citizens

2. Review the strategies for each of the five most frequent categories on your list. Implement each suggestion.

3. Keep a tally of the customers you serve over the next week. Add a "regular" category to the list. Does this actual tally match your ranking in number one above? Review any additional strategies to help you reach excellence in your customer service.

Reflections

6 RECOVERY FROM PROBLEMS AND COMPLAINTS

Everyone in the organization should be able to receive and act upon complaints. Effective complaint management can make your organization more successful. Your people should be able to address all customer complaints quickly and implement corrective measures to prevent future problems. Completing these procedures in such a way as to make a complaining customer your best friend is the focus of this chapter.

The Inevitable Complaints

No matter how hard you try, you are bound to eventually have customers who have complaints or problems. How well you handle these situations will determine whether or not the customer remains loyal to your company.

Research has shown that although one in four purchases results in some kind of problem, only 20 percent of customers will actually complain about it. The other 80 percent use problems as an excuse to go elsewhere.

Customers don't complain for three basic reasons:

- They don't believe it will do them any good.

- They don't believe anyone really cares.

- They don't know the proper channels to voice their complaints.

If a customer does complain, accept it as her way of saying she likes you. The customer who complains is giving you the opportunity to correct the problem. Studies show that people who do complain and have their problems resolved promptly, can become a company's most loyal customers.

Of those people who do complain, more than 40 percent are not satisfied with the action taken. Complaints most often involve:

- **Poor service/apathy.** The customer service employee does not live up to the customer's perceived standards for performance or projects an attitude that she just doesn't care.

- **Long waits.** The customer is forced to wait in long lines, is put on hold too long on the telephone, or has to wait for the customer service employee who is visiting or doing other things.

- **Rude service people.** The service people the customer encounters are not helpful and may even be abrasive.

- **Billing problems.** When the customer receives her bill, she discovers that it is not for the amount the service employee quoted.

- **Unknowledgeable service people.** The service employee does not know enough about the product to resolve the problem properly.

- **Difficulty with returns.** The service employee is uncooperative when the customer attempts to return merchandise.

- **The runaround.** When the customer tries to get help, she is passed from employee to employee without ever getting satisfaction.

- **Unavailability of advertised goods.** The customer goes to the store for the advertised special, only to discover that it isn't available.

Dealing with Customer Complaints

In solving a problem or complaint, remember, you and your customers basically want the same thing: to find a solution. They want to have a positive relationship with your company. If customers didn't care, they wouldn't bother to tell you that there was a problem, they just wouldn't return. When solving customer problems, try these techniques.

- **Listen.** Let the customer explain exactly what the problem is. Don't interrupt, unless it is to clarify a point.

- **Be open.** Don't begin the discussion thinking that the customer is wrong. She may be, but on the other hand, she may not be.

- **Don't say anything that may be interpreted as resistance.** Comments like, "Well, I don't know what we can do about that. Let me see," or, "I'm not sure if we can help you or not," will only aggravate her. Instead, say something like, "I'm sorry you've experienced this problem. Let me get a little additional information from you so that we can get this matter settled promptly."

- **Identify the problem.** Question the customer about the problem so that you understand exactly what is wrong.

- **Be empathetic.** Let the customer know that you understand how she feels. She will be more at ease and reassured that you can solve her problem.

- **Apologize.** If it is your mistake, say so. Acknowledging the error results in the customer developing trust in you and gives her the confidence that you are willing to solve the problem. A simple, "I'm sorry," will go a long way.

- **Ask her what you can do to resolve the problem.** Find out what the customer would like. You may find out that what she wants is actually less than the settlement you are willing to offer.

- **Be prompt.** If you have the authority to make a settlement, and what she is asking is fair, don't delay. The quicker you settle the problem, the more likely the customer is to come back. If possible, settle the problem during the initial contact. Prolonging the situation only makes the customer more frustrated, which creates additional problems.

- **Keep the customer informed.** If the solution takes a long time, be sure to call and update the customer periodically on the progress.

- **Explain the settlement clearly.** When explaining the settlement, don't leave out any details. Make sure you tell the customer exactly what she can expect.

- **Talk about future transactions.** Let the customer know that the company will try to prevent the same mistake or problem from happening in the future. This demonstrates that your company takes mistakes seriously and wants to correct them. It also tells the customer she is important to your company.

- **Say thank you.** No matter how difficult the transaction, it's a good idea to tell the customer, "Thank you." By thanking the customer, you let her know that you care and that you want to be helpful.

- **Follow up.** Your job is not finished until the customer has received the settlement you promised. Often, this settlement is issued by another employee or department. Be sure to follow through and make sure that everything happens as it is supposed to.

Responding in Writing

Not all complaints are handled face to face. Sometimes, a customer will express dissatisfaction in a letter. When this is the case, you have a little longer than usual to formulate your response. But, just like when the customer is standing in front of you, you want to respond appropriately and promptly.

When answering a complaint that has been received in the mail, follow these guidelines:

- **Read the letter carefully.** Don't just skim the letter hoping to find the problem. The only way you can respond appropriately is if you fully understand what the problem is.

- **Write the response in a friendly tone.** Keep your response friendly and positive even when you need to tell a customer you cannot give her what she has requested. Your goal is to keep her as a customer.

- **Keep it simple.** Make sure your response is perfectly clear. Write short, simple, easy-to-understand sentences.

- **Address all problems.** Make sure you answer all of the customer's concerns or problems. Although the customer's main complaint may be that she has a defective piece of equipment and wants to return it, she may also be upset about other problems that have occurred. For example, if this is the third product she has tried and they have all been defective, she may want to know why there have been so many problems.

- **Use the customer's name throughout the letter.** By repeating the customer's name, you personalize the letter.

- **Make it personal.** It's okay to use a word processor to save on time, but make sure your response does not look like a form letter. Form letters communicate a lack of honest concern and make the customer wonder about the number of complaints you receive. Personalize the letters as much as possible and sign each one individually.

- **Tell her how you plan to resolve the problem.** Let the customer know what steps will be taken to correct the problem and when.

- **Talk about future business transactions.** By ending on a positive note and talking about future business transactions with your company, you will increase the chances of the customer returning.

Sample Response Letter

Dear Ms. Smith:

In response to your letter of August 15, 1999, I am writing to let you know that I have investigated your complaint and discovered the following.

As you stated, our order department did receive your order on June 15. The order was entered into our computer immediately. Unfortunately, shortly thereafter, we experienced a power failure, and several orders were lost despite our efforts to ensure that the lost orders were re-entered; however, yours was inadvertently overlooked.

Ms. Smith, I understand that failing to receive this order on time has caused you to be inconvenienced. Please accept my apology for this error.

As you requested in your letter, we have replaced your order. To ensure that it gets to you as soon as possible, we will have it sent to you by overnight delivery service at our expense. I anticipate that it will be delivered to you on August 23.

In an effort to prevent this problem from happening in the future, we are initiating a new backup system. All operators will retain a copy of the customer's name and phone number in a special book. In the event of a similar occurrence, we can retrace our steps and ensure that everyone's order is re-entered.

Ms. Smith, we appreciate your business and the opportunity to resolve this problem. We look forward to serving your needs in the future.

Please let me know if I can ever be of assistance again.

Sincerely,

Joe Jones

Dealing with Others to Get Problems Resolved

In order to get a customer's problem resolved, you usually have to work with other people in your company. How you interact with these people will determine how quickly the problem is resolved, and how you and the company will look to the customer.

In dealing with others in your company, follow these guidelines:

- **Give the facts.** Tell the individual involved everything that you know about the problem.

- **Explain what solving it means to the customer.** For example, telling someone in your order department that Ms. Smith needs the item ordered immediately for health reasons will probably get the individual to respond quicker than simply saying, "the customer wants it delivered now." If she understands the problem, then she can relate to it better.

- **Don't be accusatory.** Regardless of the situation, don't ever approach another employee and accuse her of causing the problem, or even imply that it is her fault. Remember, your main goal is to satisfy the customer's complaint, and pointing the finger isn't going to help.

- **Suggest a solution.** Be sure to have a potential solution in mind, as well as a deadline for completing it. For example, "Since the customer has already made a trip to the store to pick up this item and it wasn't ready, she would like us to ship it to her within the next three days. Is that possible?"

- **Say thank you.** Being courteous to the people you work with is just as important as being courteous to your customers. We all like to be treated with respect. It is also essential if you expect their cooperation in the future.

Eliminating Complaints

Even in the best-run companies there are bound to be policies and procedures which can stand improvement. As the front-line person who deals directly with the customer, these problems come to your attention first.

Whenever a customer expresses a comment or complaint about a practice or procedure, write it down and pass it on to your supervisor. Putting it in writing will get results more quickly than simply telling someone. Here's why:

- When you write it down, you can make sure that you have clearly and concisely addressed all aspects of the problem.

- Writing it down puts the complaint and your response on the record. This type of documentation protects you, your company and the customer if there are any further problems with follow-up, product performance or if the customer claims no action was taken.

- Once the problem has been written down, it can easily be routed to all the parties who are involved in its correction. If you verbalize the complaint and it is passed around, it may become distorted and lose important details by the time it gets to the last person.

- Seeing it in writing will help your supervisor understand the problem more clearly. Stacks of paper are hard to ignore.

When writing the memo, provide the following information:

- The date the complaint was filed and/or the problem occurred.

- A description of what happened.

- The customer's name and phone number (if available).

- A summary of the customer's comments.

- A description of how you handled the situation.

- Your suggestion for correcting the situation.

- Your name and work phone number or extension.

Conclusion

Dealing with complaints does not have to be a negative experience. And if handled properly, they can turn a potentially lost customer into a loyal one.

In dealing with customer complaints, remember that you and the customer have the same goal in mind: to resolve the problem. Keeping this in mind will help you find a solution that is satisfactory to both the customer and your company.

Working to normalize relations with an unhappy customer is one of the highest-impact activities a service organization can undertake.

Ten Tips to Building Customer Loyalty Through Recovery

1. Never take your customers for granted.

2. Never ignore a problem or complaint.

3. Take every complaint seriously.

4. Pinpoint the complaint to an action complaint.

5. Bad systems stop good people.

6. Make recovery a point of pride ... and part of your system.

7. Good service is whatever the customer says it is.

8. Good enough never is.

9. Businesses that move quickly do more business.

10. If you don't take care of your customers, someone else will.

- Are there established procedures to handle complaints?
- Are records kept of all complaints and the actions taken?
- Does everyone who handles complaints do so effectively?
- Are complaints handled quickly?
- Do you use information gained from a complaint to improve your product or service?
- Are all levels and areas of the organization involved in handling complaints?
- How long does it take for complaints received by the mail room to reach the customer service department?
- What happens to complaints addressed to senior executives by name or title or to other departments?
- If the call is misdirected, do other employees know where to direct the call or how to handle the call?
- What do departments other than the customer service department do with incoming complaint and inquiry calls?
- Do customer service department employees have written guidelines on how to spot and what to do with serious complaints that deserve priority?
- Do all employees who receive a written or telephone complaint know what the company prioritization of complaints is and what action to take?
- Do I know how many customers are dissatisfied with the service my company provides?
- Do I know how many of these dissatisfied customers are encouraged to communicate their complaint or inquiry to my company?
- Precisely how much repeat business do my people generate from the complaints and inquiries they handle?
- If I meet a customer with a complaint or inquiry, do I know how to handle it and do I handle it?
- In the political arena, do I give the customer's needs top priority?
- Do I actively encourage my company's employees to submit ideas for improvements to effective complaint management, and do I move these ideas forward?
- Do I understand the revenue, profit and return on investment that are possible from effective complaint management?

Reflections

7 YOUR ROLE AS A CUSTOMER SERVICE EMPLOYEE

Companies don't serve customers — people do. Customers want to deal with people who are bright, perceptive and sympathetic. But, the real work of helping customers can be tiresome, frustrating and tedious.

It's easy to set impersonal service standards: How many times does the phone ring before we answer? How long is the average caller on hold? BUT, what really matters is much less tangible. What are the attitude, energy and intelligence levels on the other end of the line? Are they consistent, regardless of the time of day … or do service levels drop late in the day as fatigue sets in?

Helping you provide the same high-quality service at 5 p.m., as you did at 8 a.m., is the goal of this chapter.

Personal Characteristics of a Successful Customer Service Representative

It takes a certain kind of person to work with the public. You must be:

- Familiar with every aspect of the company

- Outgoing and helpful

- Able to think on your feet/problem-solve

- Patient and tolerant

- Flexible

- Empathetic

- Cooperative

- Enthusiastic

- Self-confident

- Resilient

Your self-image will affect the way you do your job. If you view yourself as a skilled professional, that's probably the image you will project and the way you will act. If, on the other hand, you lack confidence in your skills and abilities, others won't have confidence in you either.

Providing customer service can be a very rewarding experience. When you help someone find what they want or solve a problem, you get immediate feedback in the form of their facial expressions and their comments. But, a customer service job can also be trying. Some people have no problems meeting strangers day in, day out — in fact, they find it enjoyable. But for others, the experience can be emotionally draining.

Customer service employees have what has been termed emotionally labor-intensive jobs. In these types of jobs, you must deal with emotions and feelings, both your own and the customer's. Juggling the feelings you bring to work with those you confront on the job is not always easy.

Contact overload is the psychological term used to describe what happens to people who have problems dealing with extensive human contact. Those who suffer from it may experience a number of symptoms including fatigue, apathy, moodiness and, in some cases, hostility toward the people they have to deal with. These reactions can cause problems in an individual's personal life, as well as his professional one.

One way to reduce the pressure all these different emotions and feelings generate is to learn to compartmentalize. This means isolating feelings and emotions so you only concentrate on those that are a priority and that you can do something about. The others are put aside — compartmentalized — until later when it is appropriate to deal with them.

For instance, say your day started when you discovered the dog chewed up your new pair of shoes. Then, you went out to get into your car only to find the battery dead, which caused you to get to work late. Needless to say, by the time you arrive at work, you're not going to be in a very good mood.

As a customer service employee, however, you have to leave all of these negative feelings behind you and concentrate on positive thoughts. Tell yourself that you will deal with your personal problems when you get home. If necessary, ask your boss if you can have a few moments to collect your thoughts. Take steps to solve the problems that can be dealt with. For example, you may be able to take a few moments to call the local service station and ask them to install a new battery in your car.

Put the things you can't do anything about out of your mind. Tell yourself there is nothing you can do about your shoes. Nothing you can do will change the outcome.

First Impressions

Like it or not, people often judge us by the impressions they get in the first few seconds when we meet them. And often, the impression they get lasts a long time.

As a customer service employee who comes in contact with new people hundreds of times a day, judgments are being made about you constantly. If you understand what people react to and how they form these first impressions, you can make a conscious effort to make your first impressions good ones.

Following are some of the outward signs that determine a first impression:

- **Appearance.** How you dress conveys how you see yourself. If your clothes are neat and pressed, the customer perceives you as a detail person. If your clothes are wrinkled and mismatched, he may presume that you are just as sloppy in your work. Clothes can also project an image. If you are dressing appropriately for your business environment, the customer will assume you are a serious professional. Stay away from loud colors and flashy styles. They cause the customer to pay more attention to what you're wearing than what you're saying.

Here's a general rule of thumb to determine if you're dressed appropriately. Ask yourself, "Would I want my picture to appear in tomorrow's paper, given what I am wearing now?" If the answer is no, you are not appropriately dressed.

- **Grooming** is just as important as the clothes you wear. If your hair is greasy, you need a shave, your make-up is too heavy or applied sloppily, or you have body odor, you're not going to make a very good first impression. A good rule of thumb in grooming is to get yourself ready for work each day as if you were meeting someone for the very first time. In your job you are, in fact, meeting a lot of people for the first time.

- **Voice.** The tone of your voice also conveys a lot about you. Take the phrase, "May I help you?" Depending on your tone of voice, it can express several different meanings. If it is said in a friendly, cheerful tone, it conveys that you truly want to help the individual. If it is said in a gruff, irritated tone, it will give the customer the impression that he has interrupted you, and you don't want to be bothered.

- **Jewelry.** Be conservative in the amount and kind of jewelry that you wear. Flashy jewelry may be acceptable for social occasions, but it will not project the kind of image you want on the job. Also, as in dress, if it's too flashy or if there is too much of it, it will distract the customer from hearing what you have to say.

- **Hair styles.** Conservative is also the approach to take in hair styles. The main objective is to steer away from anything that could prove distracting to the customer. Work is not the place to experiment with extreme styles and unnatural colors.

Good Manners

When we were children, our parents taught us that good manners were important if we were to get along with others. The same magic words, "please" and "thank you," that got us a cookie as a child will earn us a loyal customer as an adult.

Just as good manners will take you a long way in this world, bad manners will hold you back. When you use good manners around your customers, you make them feel comfortable. And, as stated earlier, customers like to shop where they feel comfortable.

In addition to "please" and "thank you," there are other good manners which you can practice that will make your customers feel even more comfortable.

- **Avoid informality.** When you first meet someone, don't call him by his first name. By using a title (i.e., Mr., Ms., Mrs., Dr., etc.) you show respect. Continue to address him in that fashion until he indicates he would like you to do otherwise.

- **Avoid discussing controversial issues.** Regardless of what's going on in the world, keep your opinion on any controversial topic to yourself. Religion and politics do not belong in the workplace.

- **Don't tell jokes.** Some people may think of jokes as a good ice breaker, but jokes can backfire. What may not be offensive to you, may be to another person. Therefore, your best bet is to avoid telling jokes.

- **Watch your comments.** Be careful not to make comments that can be misconstrued as being racist, sexist or that may offend any group of people. Take, for example, a phrase like, "May I help you, dear?" If you are a male employee speaking to a female customer, she may take it as sexist. Or, if you are a female employee speaking to an older lady, she may take it as condescending.

- **Don't smoke around customers.** Although once considered acceptable, smoking is becoming increasingly unpopular among a great many people. Smoking in front of a customer who considers it objectionable may cause you to lose his business.

- **Don't chew gum or eat around customers.** Gum chewing is annoying to many people. Avoid it altogether. Also, don't bring snacks or your lunch to your customer service area. It not only makes your area look messy, but it can also put off customers. If you're eating when they approach, they may feel like they are interrupting you. Worse yet, in an effort to help them, you may begin talking while you still have food in your mouth.

Develop a Positive Attitude

Your attitude reflects how you think about something or someone. If your attitude is positive, you'll be better able to handle difficult situations. If your attitude is negative, you'll find it hard to handle even the simplest requests.

You determine whether your attitude is positive or negative. In order to develop a positive attitude, try the following:

- Realize that you have control over your attitude.

- Put bad or negative experiences behind you.

- Think about the positive aspects of your job and your life.

- If possible, avoid negative people.

Project a positive image, one that displays pride in yourself, your co-workers and your company. Part of that positive projection is monitoring closely what you say ... and how you say it. Specifically, avoid these annoying statements:

1. "It's not my job." "That's not my department." These are among the most common — and worst things — one can say to a customer.

Remember, customer service is not just a department, it's a guiding philosophy. Customers are the sole reason for a company's existence. If there's a customer on the line … it *is* your job.

2. "I'm sorry. That's the policy." Even if it is the policy, find a different way to tell the customer that. Avoid these words at all costs. The words are inflammatory and indicate that nothing can be done. Don't be one of those customer service agents who hides behind "policy." Go to bat for your customer.

3. "You'll have to call back." Statements like this imply that you really don't need the customer. Unless you are the only game in town, you do need them … so take care of them now.

4. "It's not our fault." What difference does it make whose fault it is? Focus on finding a solution. Customers are four times more likely to remain loyal to a company if a problem is handled efficiently and professionally, than if there had been no problem at all!

5. "I'm sorry, what was your name again?" Write the customer's name down immediately. Nothing makes a customer feel unimportant faster than having his name forgotten during a conversation.

6. "You're not the only customer we have, you know." True, but how rude! Treat each customer as if he were your most important customer — regardless of how much or how little he purchases from you.

Dealing with Stress

At one time or another, we all experience stress on the job. But if we learn how to deal with it, stress is less likely to take its toll on us. In order to reduce stress, we must first understand what it is and what causes it.

Stress is often the result of uncertainty and anxiety. Often, if we eliminate these factors, we eliminate much of our stress. Although external factors can play a role in stress, more often than not we bring it on ourselves.

Say, for example, you have to call a customer and tell him that you cannot provide the replacement product he requested. He was angry when he brought the broken item back, and you know he is going to blow up again. Instead of handling it first thing in the morning and getting it behind you, you put it off. You make excuses like, "I don't want to call too early in the morning, I may wake him up." At noon you're convinced you can't call because you may interrupt his lunch, and so you put it off again.

The longer you put off calling the customer, the more stress you feel. Don't allow yourself to get into this position. Face problems head-on and you will reduce much of the stress in your life.

Here are some tips on reducing other stressors.

- **Take care of one customer at a time.** Invariably, it seems like everyone comes to you with a question or problem at the same time. Don't allow yourself to get flustered. It won't help you go any faster; in fact, it will probably slow you down. Ask for help when you need it. Don't wait until the situation is totally out of control. If you see that customers are backing up, call your supervisor or a fellow worker and ask for help. If you've established a good working relationship with your fellow employees, this will be easy.

- **If a chronic problem is causing stress, see if it can be changed.** If you are experiencing stress because of a recurring situation, discuss the problem with your supervisor. Allowing it to continue will only cause you unneeded grief and upset customers.

- **Make sure customer complaints are handled.** If they're not, the customer will be calling or coming back and causing you further stress.

- **Reduce stress at home.** Off-the-job stress can filter into your work if you let it. Try to keep things in your personal life on an even keel.

- **Stay informed.** Since a good deal of stress is caused by uncertainty, you need to eliminate it from your life. If you're uncertain about any aspect of your job, ask.

- **Remember to laugh.** When it comes to stress, laughter is the best medicine. Try to find the humor in things, especially stressful situations.

- **Express yourself.** Don't keep emotions bottled up. If you're having a bad day, tell someone you feel you can confide in.

- **Vary your routine.** As the old saying goes, "Variety is the spice of life." It can also help to break up the monotony and, thus, cut down on your stress.

Managing Your Time

Stress is often caused by the feeling that there is too much to do and not enough time to get it all done. Here are some ways to help you manage your time more effectively.

- **Don't hurry.** When you rush through a task, you often make errors. Correcting errors can take you twice as long as doing the job right the first time.

- **Do the difficult jobs first.** It is human nature to put off difficult tasks for as long as we can. However, your best bet is to do them first thing in the morning when your energy level is at its height. If you put them off until later, they are in the back of your mind all day and tax your energy for other jobs.

- **Do similar jobs at the same time.** You waste time when you jump from one job to another. It breaks your concentration and, thus, takes longer. Look at all of the jobs that you have to do and then arrange them in order. For example, if you have to make some telephone calls, answer correspondence and do filing, arrange your day so that you do all of the telephone calling at the same time, the correspondence at the same time and the filing at the same time.

- **Establish goals.** Set goals that indicate when you want to have certain tasks completed. When you are successful, reward yourself with a short break or a healthy snack.

- **Maintain a list of simple tasks.** Make a list of tasks that you can do in just a few minutes. Then, when you have a little time between customers, you can start chipping away at them and get these jobs completed.

- **Avoid excuses.** It's easy to say there's not enough time to finish this project tonight, so I'll wait and start tomorrow. Somehow tomorrow never comes, and suddenly you are up against a deadline.

- **Don't procrastinate.** Jump in with both feet. Getting started is usually the hardest part of any task.

Reminders for Exceptional Customer Service

A. Customers don't talk to the company ... they talk to YOU!

B. Great service starts with a great attitude. Attitudes are contagious. Is yours worth catching?

C. Great service is in the eye of the customer.

D. Customer service is everyone's business.

E. Learn to anticipate problems. Listen to people and look for patterns ... then you'll be able to read customers' minds.

F. Don't just talk to customers — talk to management. You are the voice of the customer inside the company.

G. The deeper your knowledge, the better your judgment in handling customer calls.

H. Customers can tell you what they want. But if you listen closely, you can hear what they need.

I. It's not enough to take care of customers ... you have to care about them.

Conclusion

As the individual who determines how the customer views your company, it's important for you to make sure you display a professional, polished image at all times. Proper dress and grooming, good manners and a positive attitude will help you get a long way. Appropriate management of your time and resources adds to the aura of competence and efficiency. Also, maintaining perpetual reminders of customer service principles and avoiding thoughtless statements will help ensure your success. Developing good customer service skills will help you work more effectively with your customers and provide you with greater job satisfaction.

1. Do I always put my best foot forward?

2. Do I look and act like a customer service professional?

3. Do I monitor the guidelines for exceptional customer service?

4. Have I ever said (or implied) one of the annoying statements mentioned on pages 82 – 83? Instead, what can I say the next time that statement flashes into my head?

5. Do I serve each and every customer in a manner that will make this customer want to purchase my company's products and services again?

6. When a customer has a question, do I take the time to offer a clear and responsive explanation?

7. When many customers have the same question or problem, do I recommend improvements through the channels available to me?

8. Do I use all available tools and authority to resolve customers' questions and problems the moment they occur?

9. When a customer has a problem, do I view this as an opportunity to turn this customer into a loyal customer of my company?

10. When I have to deal with an angry customer, do I first listen calmly to allow the customer's anger to ease before proceeding with an apology and agreement on a course of action?

11. Do I actively ask customers if they are satisfied with the service, and take interest in and, if necessary, provide action on what they say?

12. Do I know how to fix or remedy the problems my customers have so that they are satisfied? Have I attended the appropriate training programs and learned all that I can about how to solve customers' problems?

13. Do I actively look for sources of potential problems and try to the best of my ability to say or do something to prevent the problems or ease the situations?

Reflections

8 WORKING AS PART OF THE CUSTOMER SERVICE TEAM

As a customer service employee, you are one part of the customer service team. The other two components are your fellow workers and the customer. In order for your transactions with customers to be successful, all three have to work together. Working together effectively is the focus of this chapter.

Co-workers as Part of the Team

Developing good rapport with the people you work with is just as important as developing good relationships with your customers. You need the help of other employees in your company if you are to service your customers effectively.

Everyone in the company works for the customer. They either work directly with the customer, or they work with the people who work with customers. Either way, everyone needs to work together in order to provide the customer with the best possible service.

As a customer service employee, you are on the front line. You are the one who deals with the customer day in, day out. Working behind the scenes are many people who support you. If they don't do their jobs, you can't do yours, and if you can't do your job, the company doesn't look good.

The philosophy behind teamwork is that everyone works together toward a common goal. If you give co-workers the recognition they deserve, they will be more willing to support you in the future.

Following are several suggestions to make sure your "teammates" work with you rather than against you.

- **Treat them with respect.** The people you work with, like you, appreciate being treated with respect. You aren't happy if someone doesn't appreciate your efforts. The same holds true for your co-workers. Don't be demanding. Even if they are your subordinates, you will get a lot further if you are polite. Be sensitive to their other responsibilities, deadlines and workload. Don't always insist they drop everything to help you.

- **Develop relationships.** When possible and if it's appropriate, develop a personal relationship, as well as a professional one, with co-workers. For example, if you know they are married and have children, ask them about their families when you see them in the hallway or in the lunchroom. Most people enjoy sharing information about their loved ones. When you show people that you truly care about them as people, they are more likely to want to help you.

- **Make allowances.** If a co-worker snaps at you or cuts you off, remember that we all have bad days. Don't let her bad day interfere with the job you have to do. Consider this example:

| Customer Service Employee: | "Jim, I'm calling about the Bradley order. When will it be finished?" |
| Jim: | "I don't know. We have so much going on down here, there is no way to get it all done." |

Instead of demanding that Jim answer your question (which probably won't get you very far), you can use empathy and understanding. An effective response, therefore, might be:

| Customer Service Employee: | "I've heard you guys are really overloaded. Is there someone else in your department who has a few minutes to check this for me? I told the customer I would call her back this afternoon." |

With this type of attitude, Jim is more likely to respond favorably to your request, and you get the information you need.

- **Don't assign blame.** Everybody makes mistakes. You don't appreciate being reminded of a mistake that you made, and neither do your co-workers. Stress the positive and avoid the negative. For example, if a co-worker forgot to place an order, don't mention that fact. Just ask, "When do you think we can get it in?"

- **Play by the rules.** Know who you should turn to when there is a problem. Going around a co-worker or over her head isn't going to make you a friend. When you need that person's help the next time, she is liable to be uncooperative.

- **Say thank you.** When a fellow employee helps you, say "thank you." It may be part of her job, but everyone likes to feel appreciated. The next time you are in a bind, that individual will be more likely to help you out — even if it's not part of her job.

- **Praise others.** If a customer thanks you for your efficiency and help, be sure to mention the other people involved. For example, you might say, "If it weren't for the people in shipping who called in your order right away, we never could have gotten it here on time. They really go out of their way to help our customers." This kind of response makes you and the company look good.

- **Show that you're part of the team.** If a fellow employee comes to you for help, lend a hand whenever you can. If you are willing to help when she needs it, she will be more likely to reciprocate.

- **Give credit.** If a co-worker goes above and beyond the call of duty, let her supervisor know what she has done and how it helped to satisfy the customer's needs. This kind of credit will eventually get back to the employee in the form of praise or maybe even a raise. Once again, if she finds out you were responsible, she will be grateful.

- Let your co-workers know that they are an important part of the team. As the person on the front line, you receive immediate feedback from your customers. Your co-workers, however, seldom get this kind of recognition. When a customer expresses pleasure with the way a job was handled and a fellow employee had a part, be sure to let her know. For example, you might say, "Sally, you should have seen the expression on Mrs. Jones' face when she stopped in and found her order had arrived in just one day. She was so appreciative that she placed another, even bigger, order. We couldn't have done it without your help. Thanks."

Customers as Part of Your Team

In addition to the people you work with who are part of your team, there is another member you may not even be aware of — the customer. Customers like to be involved in the service process. That's why more and more we are seeing self-service stores and gas stations popping up across the nation.

Contrary to popular belief, the main reason customers pump their own gas, eat in cafeterias and go to self-service grocery stores is not price. Research shows that people choose self-service businesses because they want to be part of the process and they feel a sense of accomplishment in doing it themselves.

As a service employee, you can capitalize on these needs. When helping your customers, involve them in the process.

- **Ask them for their opinions.** Show your customer several items and ask her for her reaction. For example, you may say, "I think the blue one looks nice on you. Which one do you like?"

- **Ask them to tell you about similar products they have used.** For example, if the customer is looking at new stereo equipment, you may ask her questions such as, "What other brands have you purchased? What did you think of their performance?"

- **Involve them in the problem-solving process.** When there is a problem, ask customers what you can do about it to make it right. If they have a say in the matter, then they become part of the solution.

Conclusion

As a customer service employee, you are part of a team. If the company is to be a winner, then the entire team — you, your fellow employees and the customer — will have to work together. If you don't, not just one of you will lose, but all of you will.

Like customers, your fellow employees want to be treated with courtesy and respect. If you make an effort to build relationships with your colleagues and co-workers, you will find that they are willing to help out if you are in a bind.

1. How would you describe your customer service team?

2. On a scale of 1 – 10 (10 being great), how would you rate your interactions with:

   a. Co-workers within your department

   b. Colleagues throughout your organization

   c. Customers

3. How would each of them rate you?

4. Complete this statement: My vision of a team that works is …

   Ask other team members to complete the same statement. Compare your responses.

5. Outline two things you can do to improve your teamwork with each group:

   Co-workers in department

   1.

   2.

   Colleagues all over company

   1.

   2.

   Customers

   1.

   2.

Reflections

9 THE CUSTOMER SERVICE SUPERVISOR

Whether you're currently a supervisor or hope to be one someday, understanding the responsibilities and focus of a customer service supervisor can teach you a great deal about the teamwork concept. As a supervisor, it's your job to find the best possible people for the job. And once you've found them, you need to keep them motivated to provide exceptional service to your customers.

Some people have negative feelings about service jobs. Some people think of a service employee as the "low man on the totem pole." Others, particularly those whose jobs involve physical labor, see service jobs as "soft" or "easy." Actually, neither one could be further from the truth.

The customer service employee has one of the most important jobs in the company. It is not an exaggeration to say that how well the customer service employee does his job has a significant impact on the job security of all employees. If a company loses many customers because of poor service, then the future of the entire company is threatened.

The role of the customer service supervisor in finding, hiring, training and overseeing the performance of the customer service team is the focus of this chapter.

Hiring the Right People

Finding the right people for customer service positions can be tricky. You need to find individuals who work well with people, are organized, quick thinkers, empathetic and enthusiastic.

The first step is to do a thorough job audit to accurately assess the specifics of the responsibilities to be fulfilled. Elements of a job audit include:

- Specifically what are the duties required to complete the job?

- What tools, services and/or accommodations are needed to complete these duties?

- Who supervises the employee in this position?

- With which other people does this person interact — in and out of the organization?

- Can all duties be completed in the time allotted?

- What formal training does a person need to perform this job satisfactorily?

- What are the evaluation criteria and process?

The second step is to analyze the specific skills needed to fill the job.

- Make a list of the skills the person needs to be successful. Which skills must the person already possess, and what training will the company offer to expand his existing skill base? Does the job require any special technical skills? For example, if he is going to be working with computers, is a knowledge of computers important, or do you plan to teach him what he needs to know after he has been hired?

- Determine the specific qualities the individual needs to have. All customer service employees need to be friendly, outgoing and understanding. But are there other qualities specific to this job that they need? For example, if the job is for a travel agent, maybe you need to find someone who can help customers visualize the perfect vacation.

- Conduct an informal survey. Visit with your customers to find out what qualities they value in service people. What do they feel is important?

The Interview

Review your job audit before you start interviewing. Be sure you've identified in writing exactly what the individual will be expected to do.

When you meet with the applicant, your job is to give him an accurate idea of what the job will entail and what your exact expectations are. This is also the time to make a preliminary judgment about how well, or if, he will fit into your organization and how capable he is of doing the job. In the interview consider the following:

- What is your first impression? As a customer service employee, customers will judge this individual on the first impression he makes on them. Look at the applicant as the customer would. Is his dress appropriate? Is he well-groomed? Confident?

- How well does he express himself? An important part of any customer service job is communication. How freely does the individual communicate with you? Are his responses to your questions well-thought-out? Does he have a good command of the language?

- Is he friendly and outgoing? As part of the customer service team, he will have to get along with fellow employees as well as the customers. Does he have the necessary people skills to do that?

- What do his nonverbal clues tell you? Does he seem calm and relaxed, or is he sitting on the edge of his chair fidgeting? Was his handshake firm, or did it show hesitancy? Does he look you in the eye when he speaks?

- Does he have ambition? Is he the type of individual who will be able to move up in the company?

- Is he bilingual? If you live in an area where there are a lot of foreign-born residents, knowing a second language could be a plus.

- Does he have the necessary writing skills? If he is going to be responsible for answering correspondence, writing memos or putting together reports, make sure that he has good, solid writing skills. Some people are good talkers, but have a hard time expressing themselves in writing.

Ask the Right Questions

In addition to your overall impression, you will want to ask questions which indicate how the person will handle various job situations. A good way to do this is to ask him to participate in a role-playing exercise.

Since customer service employees must deal with a lot of different people, some who may even be difficult, use a problem scenario. Play the part of several difficult people, such as the angry customer, the argumentative customer and the nontalker, to see how he responds to each.

Question him about his past work experience. Why did he leave his last job? What did he like most and least about that job? If one of the things he disliked was answering the phone, and that will be an important part of this job, he may not be the person you are looking for.

Ask him why he would like to work for your company. This will give you some idea of what he is looking for. Are good company benefits the most important thing to him, or is he looking for a company where he feels there is room for advancement? If he wants to move ahead, find out how long he is willing to wait. He may see this job as a way to get his foot in the door. If he anticipates being promoted in a year and you know there is no possibility for advancement for at least five, you need to let him know up front. Otherwise, he will become dissatisfied, and you will be looking for another employee.

Find out how he views the role of the customer service employee. Is he sensitive to the importance of meeting a customer's needs, making the extra effort to build relationships with customers, and building and maintaining good relationships with fellow employees?

A good final question might be how he envisions the job he is applying for. For example, he may view the job as an opportunity to meet fun and interesting people. If the job actually entails sitting behind a desk and taking orders over the phone, he may be sorely disappointed once he gets into the job, and you will be disappointed that he doesn't work out.

In addition to asking the right questions, it's important to listen carefully to his answers. Although you should have a set of prepared questions to ask, don't limit what you ask to what you've prepared. Listen carefully to his responses and then use them as a springboard to further questioning.

Getting the Straight Scoop

It's important to assess the veracity and completeness of the information provided by the interviewee. Use these statements and questions to aid in your assessment.

"When I talk with your former boss, what will he or she tell me about ... ? (Start with easy questions.) I don't like surprises! Is there anything in your past jobs you would like to explain now before I talk with your former supervisors?"

"We feel it is important to talk directly with your last two supervisors. Do you have any problems with that?" (Watch closely for reaction and be sure to get supervisors' names and phone numbers.)

Note: A bad reference is as hard to find as a good employee.

Provide the Applicant with a Job Description

Before the first applicant ever walks through the door, you need to write a job description based on the job audit you've completed. The job description should be given to applicants at the interview. It will help you explain the job and demonstrate that you have a clear understanding of the type of person you are looking for.

Here is a sample job description for a customer service representative at a computer store:

JOB TITLE:	Customer Service Representative
REPORTS TO:	Store Manager
PRIMARY FUNCTION:	To work with customers to sell computer systems best suited to their needs.
DUTIES AND RESPONSIBILITIES:	
Verbal communication:	Must possess good speaking and listening skills in order to assess customers' needs.
Writing skills:	Must be able to compose follow-up letters to customers to reiterate recommendations.
Telephone skills:	Must be able to effectively communicate with customers using the telephone.
Attention to details:	Must be detail-oriented. Individual needs to be able to keep accurate records of recommendations made to customers and prices quoted. Must have above-average organizational skills which allow the employee to follow up with customers in a timely manner.
Computer skills:	Must have basic knowledge of computers and be willing to take 40 hours of classes to further advance knowledge.

In developing the job description, be sure to list the skills needed in order of importance.

Matching the Applicant to the Job:

- Education: Tell me about your formal education. What subjects did you enjoy/dislike?

- Work experience: Explain the primary responsibilities of your current/most recent job.

- Skills and aptitudes: Tell me how you would successfully complete XYZ task.

- Attitudes and personality: Describe the ideal working conditions for you. What kinds of experiences have you had as a customer in a (business like yours)?

- Career/occupational objectives: Tell me what interests you about this job?

- Team view: My vision of a team that works is ...

Selecting the Right Employee for the Job

Even though we would like to think that we always choose the best-qualified person for the job, it's not always easy to be totally objective. We all have our likes and dislikes, and these have a way of creeping into our subconscious even when we're hiring staff.

Seriously consider those who ...

- Show proven capability

- Show achievements, not just functions

- Demonstrate interest in the job

- Radiate enthusiasm

- Ask logical questions

- Arrive on time

- Appear to get along with co-workers

- Are well-mannered, not condescending

- Show loyalty to former employers

- Give employer(s) adequate notice

- Show how past experience/special knowledge will benefit your organization

Be wary of candidates who ...

- Quit a job without adequate notice

- Accept terms and then try to "up the offer"

- Are rude to your receptionist

- Arrive late for interviews

- Dress inappropriately/are poorly groomed

- Supply no verifiable references

- Appear angry during the interview

- Seem to know little about former employers

- Lie about material factors

- Are overqualified (except older candidates)

- Reveal confidential information

The most important thing is to try to find someone who is as closely matched to the job as possible. Even though your decision is bound to be somewhat subjective, it is important to make sure that the person you hire has all of the basic skills and abilities that you need. Don't look at an individual and think, "He'll change," or, "We can probably teach him to be more outgoing." There are some skills that can't be taught.

Your Role as Supervisor

As a supervisor, your role is to oversee the work of your subordinates. You need to ensure that they are not only doing their job properly, but that they are loyal to the company and remain motivated.

Supervision can be tricky, especially if you have no previous experience. As a supervisor, it is your job to delegate work, make sure the job is done right, solve problems and motivate your employees.

Instead of taking the time to explain to an employee how to do a job the proper way, you may be tempted to think, "do it myself." Avoid this line of thinking. Sometimes it is easier to do a job yourself, but that's not your function. Your job is to get the most out of the people who work for you.

Practice hands-off management as much as possible, and hands-on management as much as necessary.

Being a good supervisor means training employees to do the job and then making sure they get it done. Some specific training needs/issues to consider include:

- Questioning: open vs. closed

- Fact-finding

- Product knowledge

- Company knowledge

- Processing procedures

- Empowerment — authority and limits

- Tone/Manner

- Listening skills

- Computer downtime procedures

- Sales techniques

- Problem-solving procedures

- Stress management

- Escalation procedures — problem resolution

Dealing with Performance Concerns

When faced with a performance concern, coaching for success is often appropriate. This involves six steps:

- Establish the purpose of the discussion and its importance

- Discuss and clarify details about the situation

- Agree on what needs to be accomplished

- Discuss alternatives for achieving success

- Seek agreement on specific action(s) to be taken

- Express confidence and set a follow-up date

It sounds easy, but it is definitely not. Being in a leadership position is seldom easy; and being in a leadership position when corrective action is required is very difficult. When you find yourself in that position — and all supervisors eventually do — keep these things in mind:

- Have a plan of action ready

- Begin on a pleasant note

- Advise the employee of the meeting in advance

- State the problem clearly

- Avoid interruptions and don't permit distractions

- Avoid using absolutes

- Cite earlier discussions of the employee's problem

- Be aware of theatrics

- Find out what motivates the employee

- Maintain eye contact

- Don't let the employee sidetrack you

- Ask for feedback

- Use specific examples from work situations

- Don't apologize

- Avoid relying on rumors

- Stress the positive

- Keep the discussion on target

- Stay calm

- Be aware of your body language

- Reverse roles with the employee

- Maintain control of the situation

- Don't make promises

Lead by example: The role of a leader is to inspire others to follow.

Another important aspect of your supervisory position is your status as role model. Your employees (like your children) watch you more than they listen. It is your job to model the type of customer-focused service you expect from your employees. Excellent customer service cannot be achieved without excellent employee relations. Treat your employees the way you want them to treat your customers.

Celebrating Customer-centered Success

- One key to employee motivation is to make work feel like play. (Most play involves a challenging goal, an effort to reach it, and deep satisfaction at getting even a little closer.)

- Be generous with praise. Use "One-Minute Praisings."

- Celebrate successes: big, small, individual, group.

- Frequent and varied contests to fight boredom and routine (sales, attendance).

- Provide instant recognition.

- Recognize and reward the development of all skills — even if not specifically related to job function.

- Identify unique motivators for each of your employees to individualize recognitions for excellence. What are that person's interests, hobbies, favorite restaurants, music preferences, etc.? Focus on fun, laughter and positive reinforcement, rather than on monetary rewards.

Visionary leaders give their people the opportunity to participate in great success.

Conclusion

Understanding the role of the customer service supervisor is important if you are going to be an effective member of the team. It's also a good idea to have a true sense of what the job entails in case the employee has aspirations of moving into management.

In order to hire the right people for the job, it's necessary to do some preparation. If you prepare properly, it will pay off in trusted, loyal employees. Your supervisory responsibilities are just beginning. Proper training, oversight, motivation, discipline and leading by example are essential traits.

Superstar customer service supervisors unfailingly do nine things:

- Find and keep excellent people

- Really know their customers well

- Focus on vision

- Be ETDBW (easy to do business with)

- Create competence, confidence and loyalty

- Involve and empower

- Recognize, reward and celebrate success

- Set the tone and lead by example

- Make a commitment to their commitment

1. Do performance standards in my department gear performance to deliver service as a number one priority, and do they inspire exceptional satisfaction?

2. Do I know why customers are dissatisfied with our service? What is the cost to correct?

3. Do I know exactly how many of our customers are dissatisfied with our service and how much it costs to handle?

4. How many days in the last year have I actually spent working as a customer contact employee in my company?

5. Do I regularly know how my customers perceive my company's products and services?

6. Do I regularly know how my company's employees perceive my company's products and services?

7. Do I actively volunteer for projects, assignments and positions that will allow me to contribute and help me develop new skills?

8. For each decision I make or each customer contact I have, do I try to consider how it fits with the company's overall goals, directions and service strategy?

9. Do my team and I pay attention to actual service delivery and always know what our service levels are?

10. Do I read and study quality assurance reports, audit reports and customer service reports about my areas of responsibility and take immediate action to solve problems and improve service?

Reflections

11. Am I able to discuss customer satisfaction and actual service delivery in specific financial terms?

- Do I manage, lead and treat my staff as I want to see our customers treated?

- Do I encourage and listen to ideas from service delivery and service support personnel, and help to refine, quantify and cost justify them? Do I bring these ideas to the attention of the decision-makers in the organization in the ways most likely to gain approval?

- Do I make every effort to fully understand corporate goals, directions and strategies and to execute them in concert with their intent?

- Do I provide opportunities for service delivery and service support personnel to perform their jobs well and to feel some initiative and positive rewards in service-related situations?

- Do I schedule myself regularly to work as a customer contact employee in my company, to speak to my company's customers and to listen to service delivery and service support personnel?

- How many days in the last year have I actually spent working as a customer contact employee in my company?

12. How many hours in the last 12 months have I spent actually talking to my company's customers?

Reflections

Hiring

1. Do I have an accurate job description for each position for which I must hire people?

2. Do I have an accurate specification of the skills needed to do the job?

3. Am I using the most effective recruitment methods to attract the right applicants?

4. Do my interviews ask "what if" questions and allow the applicant to demonstrate his or her service skills and attitudes?

5. Do I use all of the available ways to assess applicants, such as reference checking, employment agencies and psychological evaluation?

6. Am I able to attractively explain the salary and benefits?

7. Do I have sound criteria upon which to base my selections?

8. Do I actively seize any opportunity to speak to prospective applicants in social or business situations and encourage them to apply for jobs in my company or organization?

9. Do I keep in touch with competitive salary and benefit offerings and make justified recommendations for change when appropriate?

10. Do I assign the recruitment and selection process the right priority so that I am not simply hiring warm bodies?

Reflections

Training

1. Do I enroll my employees and myself in all company training courses for which we are eligible and that are appropriate?

2. Do I rearrange schedules and priorities so that my employees and I can participate fully in courses we attend?

3. Do I discuss the course objectives and their importance with my employees before they attend a course, so they are prepared positively to take maximum advantage of the course?

4. When employees return from a training course, do I review what has been learned and discuss how it will apply on the job?

5. Do I send new employees to training courses or give them adequate on-the-job training before asking them to perform their new job or serve customers?

6. Am I familiar with what is taught to my employees in company training courses and do I support and reinforce the training given? If there is a procedure/technique being taught that I don't agree with, do I try to resolve this disagreement with the training department?

7. Do I actively contribute to the design and content of training programs for my employees?

8. Do I encourage my employees to develop themselves?

9. When my employees face a new procedure, service, product or decision, do I try to explain and help them fully understand it?

10. Do I have and follow an action plan for my own development?

Reflections

Leadership

1. Do I understand my company's service strategy and the role my team and I play in it?

2. Do I actively promote team spirit?

3. Do the policies and procedures within my area support the service strategy?

4. Do I devote time to explaining decisions to my staff when sending them to training programs in order to develop their conceptual skills?

5. Do my employees have the right tools and levels of authority to perform their jobs in line with my company's service strategy?

6. Do I regularly review the programs in my area for rewarding and recognizing employees?

7. Do I listen to employee ideas about service offerings and customer education in my area of responsibility, and ensure they are carried forward?

8. Do I do everything within my power to always create opportunities for people to deliver superior service?

9. What decisions have I made and actions have I taken in the last year to create the opportunity for people to deliver superior service?

10. What are the first three steps I need to take to improve the customer focus of my group?

Reflections

10 EXCEPTIONAL CUSTOMER SERVICE: A RECAP

As a customer service employee, you have one of the most important jobs in your company. The perception your customers have of your company is due in large part to the way they see you.

In today's service-oriented economy, building strong customer relationships and providing top-notch service are viewed as the only ways companies can survive. You cannot, therefore, take your responsibility lightly.

Your job as a customer service employee is to determine the customer's needs and then meet those needs. What do customers want? Generally, the motivating factor is not price, it's good service. You may feel that you are providing good service, but that really doesn't matter if your customers don't think so.

Although it's impossible to lump all customers together, there are some basic qualities that customers want when they choose a company to do business with. The qualities that most customers look for when seeking good service are:

- Courtesy

- Prompt attention

- Reliability

- Empathy

- Personal attention

- Responsiveness

- Dependability

- Promptness

- Employee competence

- Politeness

As a service employee, a major part of your job involves communication. Communication is more than a simple dialogue between two people. It involves nonverbal communication, listening and speaking. All are skills you need to develop if you are going to communicate effectively with your customers.

Listening involves more than simply hearing words. You need to listen both with your ears and your mind. If you don't fully understand what individuals want, you can't meet their needs or expectations.

Once you've heard what individuals have said, it's imperative to be sure that you understand it. You can verify this by asking the appropriate questions.

Communicating with a customer by phone is different than communicating in person. You can't rely on body language to help you determine what the customer is thinking. When communicating by phone, there are some basic courtesies that will help make the transaction more pleasant. These include:

- Answering the phone within three rings

- Greeting the customer appropriately

- Speaking in a clear, audible tone

- Giving the customer your full attention

- Using the hold button when you need to check on something

- Never leaving the customer on hold for more than 60 seconds

In all forms of communication, it is important that you express yourself well. The way in which you say things and the words that you use can say more or less than you anticipate.

Throughout your career you will encounter thousands of different customers. Most will be easy to deal with. There are some who are difficult to deal with and can cause you problems if you let them.

The important thing in dealing with difficult people is to try to understand what motivates them to behave the way they do. Angry, argumentative and unhappy customers often act the way they do because of external forces. Understanding this will help you deal with them better.

One essential thing to remember in dealing with all customers is to keep your emotions in check. Don't allow yourself to get upset, regardless of the situation. If you keep a cool head and talk in a calm, rational voice, the individual will begin doing the same thing. The other thing to remember is to concentrate on what customers are saying, not how they are saying it. You both have the same goal in mind: to find a solution to the problem.

When dealing with difficult people, look at them as a challenge. If you think of them as a problem, it's going to ruin your day. But, if you see them as presenting a unique, problem-solving opportunity, you will find your job exciting and rewarding.

Successfully handling complaints is another challenging aspect of your job. As the front-line person in your company, you are the one exposed to most of the complaints. Think of complaining customers as your friends. The reason they complain is because they like you and want to help you do a better job. Research tells us that only one in 15 or 20 people complains. Those who don't just go somewhere else.

What customers complain about:

- Poor service
- Long waits

- Rude service people

- Billing problems

- Unknowledgeable service people

- Difficulty with returns

- Getting the runaround

- Unavailability of advertised goods

- Problems with products

Studies show that prompt attention to a customer's complaint will help win you a loyal customer. Since it costs five times as much to attract a new customer as it does to retain a current customer, it's well worth the effort it takes to try and find an equitable solution.

In dealing with customer complaints, the most important thing is to listen carefully to what the customers are telling you, and then respond to each of the concerns. Don't ignore anything.

Customers also want the customer service employee to show empathy. They want to feel like somebody truly understands how they feel. Responding to written complaints is a little different than dealing with customers face to face. You have longer to formulate a response, but you don't get the immediate feedback that you do when the individual is standing before you.

As in face-to-face communication, you want to ensure that you know exactly what the problem is, keep the exchange friendly and address all of the customer's concerns and problems.

If the same complaints occur again and again, you may want to review your company's policies and procedures to determine if they need to be changed. If so, write a memo to your supervisor explaining the problem and suggest a solution if possible.

In solving customer complaints and problems, it is often necessary to work with others in your company. Developing a good relationship with them ahead of time is an effective tool in accomplishing your goal.

The bottom line in customer relations is to keep the customer happy. How can you do that? The best way is to follow the Golden Rule of "Do Unto Others." Think about how you want to be treated. Chances are good that the things you want as a consumer are the same things your customers want.

Customers also want their experience to be as easy as possible. It's your job to make sure that it is. If you or the company has made a mistake, admit it openly. Don't try to hide it. Doing so only makes matters worse. Accept responsibility for what has happened, discuss possible solutions and get the problem resolved promptly.

As a customer service employee, you are part of a very important team. This team consists of you, your co-workers and the customer. All are vital to the success of the company. All members of the team want to be treated with respect. If you do so, chances are you will all be winners.

It takes a special person to work with the public. You have to know not only your customer, but also yourself. You must be confident and demonstrate a positive attitude at all times, even when everything seems to go wrong.

Since most of your encounters with customers will be relatively brief, it's important that you project a positive first impression. This is accomplished not only by what you say, but also by the way you dress and act.

In dealing with customers, you need to show them your best side all the time. There is no room in customer service for emotional outbursts or rude behavior. Regardless of what has happened outside the job, you need to check your negative thoughts at the door when you come to work.

Providing good customer service benefits you and your company. If customers are happy, they will continue to do business with your company, your company will make a profit and you gain increased job security. If you don't satisfy your customers' needs, they will stop doing business with your company, your company will lose money and your job will be in jeopardy.

When it comes to working with customers, make every effort to go the extra mile. They will notice the effort and, in the long run, you will benefit.

Being excellent at what we do makes doing it a pleasure.

RECOMMENDED READING

- Carlow, Peggy, and Vasudha Kathleen Deming. *The Big Book of Customer Service Training Games: Quick, Fun Activities for Training Customer Service Reps, Salespeople, and Anyone Else Who Deals With Customers*, 1998.

- Cleveland, Brad, and Julia Maben. *Call Center Management on Fast Forward: Succeeding in Today's Dynamic Inbound Environment*, 1998.

- Crandall, Rick. *Celebrate Customer Service: Insider Secrets*, 1999.

- Friedman, Nancy J. *Customer Service Nightmares: 100 Tales of the Worst Experiences Possible and How They Could Have Been Fixed*, 1998.

- Gitomer, Jeffrey. *Customer Satisfaction Is Worthless, Customer Loyalty Is Priceless: How to Make Customers Love You, Keep Them Coming Back and Tell Everyone They Know*, 1998.

- Harps, Leslie Hansen. *Motivating Customer Service Employees*, 1998.

- Hiebeler, Robert. *Best Practices: Building Your Business with Customer-Focused Solutions*, 1998.

- Sewell, Carl, and Paul Brown. *Customers for Life: How to Turn That One-Time Buyer into a Lifetime Customer*, 1998.

- Shelton, Ken. *Best of Class: Building a Customer Service Organization*, 1998.

- Zemke, Ron, and John A. Woods. *Best Practices in Customer Service*, 1999.

INDEX

Buy any 3, get 1 FREE!

Get a 60-Minute Training Series™ Handbook FREE ($14.95 value)*
when you buy any three. See back of order form for full selection of titles.

These are helpful how-to books for you, your employees and co-workers. Add to your library. Use for new-employee training, brown-bag seminars, promotion gifts and more. Choose from many popular titles on a variety of lifestyle, communication, productivity and leadership topics. Exclusively from National Press Publications.

DESKTOP HANDBOOK ORDER FORM

Ordering is easy:

1. Complete both sides of this Order Form, detach, and mail, fax or phone your order to:

   Mail: National Press Publications
   P.O. Box 419107
   Kansas City, MO 64141-6107

   Fax: 1-913-432-0824
   Phone: 1-800-258-7248
   Internet: www.natsem.com

2. Please print:

Name_____ Position/Title _____

Company/Organization_____

Address_____City _____

State/Province_____ZIP/Postal Code _____

Telephone (____)_____ Fax (____) _____

Your e-mail: _____

3. Easy payment:

☐ Enclosed is my check or money order for $_____ (total from back).
   Please make payable to National Press Publications.

Please charge to:
☐   MasterCard   ☐ VISA   ☐ American Express

Credit Card No. _____ Exp. Date_____

Signature_____

• •

MORE WAYS TO SAVE:

SAVE 33%!!! BUY 20-50 COPIES of any title ... pay just $9.95 each ($11.25 Canadian).

SAVE 40%!!! BUY 51 COPIES OR MORE of any title ... pay just $8.95 each ($10.25 Canadian).

* $20.00 in Canada

Buy 3, get 1 FREE!
60-MINUTE TRAINING SERIES™ HANDBOOKS

TITLE	RETAIL PRICE	QTY	TOTAL
8 Steps for Highly Effective Negotiations #424	$14.95		
Assertiveness #4422	$14.95		
Balancing Career and Family #4152	$14.95		
Common Ground #4122	$14.95		
Delegate for Results #4592	$14.95		
The Essentials of Business Writing #4310	$14.95		
Everyday Parenting Solutions #4862	$14.95		
Exceptional Customer Service #4882	$14.95		
Fear & Anger: Slay the Dragons … #4302	$14.95		
Fundamentals of Planning #4301	$14.95		
Getting Things Done #4112	$14.95		
How to Coach an Effective Team #4308	$14.95		
How to De-Junk Your Life #4306	$14.95		
How to Handle Conflict and Confrontation #4952	$14.95		
How to Manage Your Boss #493	$14.95		
How to Supervise People #4102	$14.95		
How to Work With People #4032	$14.95		
Inspire & Motivate: Performance Reviews #4232	$14.95		
Listen Up: Hear What's Really Being Said #4172	$14.95		
Motivation and Goal-Setting #4962	$14.95		
A New Attitude #4432	$14.95		
The New Dynamic Comm. Skills for Women #4309	$14.95		
The Polished Professional #4262	$14.95		
The Power of Innovative Thinking #428	$14.95		
The Power of Self-Managed Teams #4222	$14.95		
Powerful Communication Skills #4132	$14.95		
Present With Confidence #4612	$14.95		
The Secret to Developing Peak Performers #4692	$14.95		
Self-Esteem: The Power to Be Your Best #4642	$14.95		
Shortcuts to Organized Files & Records #4307	$14.95		
The Stress Management Handbook #4842	$14.95		
Supreme Teams: How to Make Teams Work #4303	$14.95		
Thriving on Change #4212	$14.95		
Women and Leadership #4632	$14.95		

Sales Tax		
Sales Tax All purchases subject to state and local sales tax. Questions? Call **1-800-258-7248**	Subtotal	$
	Add 7% Sales Tax *(Or add appropriate state and local tax)*	$
	Shipping and Handling *($3 one item; 50¢ each additional item)*	$
	TOTAL	$

08/01